Cooking on The Piste

A Ski Chalet Cookbook

By James McBride

& Mark Chetham

An imprint of

flightsofpassion.com

James McBride & Mark Chetham

Max Bochaton, très populaire et estimé, laissera le souvenir d'un homme au grand coeur.

DEDICATION

For Max Bochaton
- died 17th August 1994
in a plane crash
near Aosta in the Alps

CONTENTS

Some skiers are always pushing the boundaries...

James McBride & Mark Chetham

ACKNOWLEDGMENTS

Berni Chetham, Natalie McBride, Susan Gordon Tait,
Mollie McBride, Hannah McBride, Amanda Richardson,
Angela Anderson, Terry & Carol Batty, Jane Hurst,
Ashley Wilkes, Steve Kadera, Sarah Ghidouche,
Peter X, Louis McBride, Gill McBride, Pip Crocker,
Jessica Gardner, Uncle Willi, Yvonne Pass,
Madame Boufar, Wendy Constantinis, Bob Sutcliff,
Stan Vines, Arthur Charles Robinson, David Field esq,
Susan Reed-Marnoch, Amanda Proctor,
Alan Nicholson, Bob Dixon, Chris Mann,
Kate Baldry, Shiraz Graham, Martin & Helena Scott,
David Steele, Christine Smeulders, Steve Berg,
Victoria Dearlove, Rachel Sole, John King,
Jim Newman, Andreas Taxakis, Kate Fenton, Jim Gilchrist,
David White, Natassa Futadaki, Dinos Molyndris,
Dimitris Kehayas, Patrice Galinier, "Croque", Jeremy Pratt,
Gary Crates, Maroin Mekaoui, Ros & John Yarrow,
Yorgos Stabelos, Eleni Megas, Pamela Noyes,
Despina Crook, Maria Taksanakis, Tracy Murphy,
Jeremy Diack, Deborah Croasdell, Margaret Evans,
Stephanie Lightbound, Jose Augusto, Rick Aitken,
Marion Trognon, Benedict Arnold, Claudio Palma

And Max Bochaton... of course there was always Max...

Ski Chalet Fireside
January 2010

1 CHALET LOUIS COOKBOOK

The idea of catering for a whole family after a hard day on the slopes is exactly why hotels and catered chalets have their rightful place in the world of family and group ski holidays. However, easier access to ski resorts via low cost airlines and increasing numbers of rental properties will put many people in uncharted territory; the do-it-yourself, fly by the seat of your pants type!

James and Mark were quietly sharing a little après ski beverage when the conversation came up. "I've got an idea" chirped James. As with most of James' ideas Mark thought to himself, *Ahah! this will be interesting.* James continued "Why not share all our experience with other people to help them out, a kind of hints and tips to get you through the ski holiday, feeding everybody well with the minimum of fuss and expense?" His infectious smile and can do attitude was met with an unusually quizzical look, "Yes that's MY idea" replied Mark, "did I share it with you last night after one too many Vins Chaud...?"

So it came to pass, that these two ski buddies with over 20 years of experience of making food imaginative and nourishing, soothing aching limbs at the end of the day or reviving energy levels at lunchtime, had been thinking along very similar lines. Now they would share their ideas and have some fun doing it. As both families have grown up with skiing holidays, the ideas have adapted and the following selection of recipes is flexible enough to suit just about any situation, and save hundreds of Pounds/Euros in the process!

The Authors

1st September 2015

"If you can read... you can cook!"

These words were a favourite phrase of my father and he was serious. His name was Louis and when it came to naming the Ski Chalet I had built in the French Alps in 1989, (three years after his death), the choice seemed obvious.

My dad was actually a very good cook himself and my brothers and I always recall with fondness the times when mum went into hospital to have another baby, knowing that dad was going to be our personal chef for the week – Hurrah! Not that mum's cooking was bad you understand, but dad really did make a big effort to impress us with his culinary skills. It must have worked because here I am many years later relating how sharp he was in the kitchen.

Later on, when we four sons were in our teens, dad would again feature in the kitchen at home and he used to have his favourite recipes which he cooked. We always remember that he made a wonderful Terrine (coarse Pâté) which involved a great amount of messing about mixing and stirring to obtain the correct mix of ingredients with the perfect consistency. He was a Consultant Orthodontist by trade and his work was quite demanding. We certainly all knew about it when he came home at the end of a particularly difficult week. He wouldn't say much, but he would throw himself into his Terrine making like a man possessed! The result of his efforts was delicious and in the process he had worked off all his aggression.

*

Sometime in June 1989 I took my Mum to the French Alps for a weekend. We landed in Geneva, one of my favourite airports and drove up into the mountains – the scenery took our breath away. It wasn't just a weekend jaunt, we were on a mission. In my bag I had a selection of skiing brochures and I wanted to buy a ski chalet.

I had a few ideas in my head. It had to be within easy driving distance of Geneva and it must be somewhere pleasant to go in the other three seasons, not just in the winter. Now anyone who knows the French ski resorts, will also know their reputation for being built at high altitude, above the tree line, composed mostly of huge characterless blocks of apartments. Not what I was looking for...

There was one little ski resort that featured in the holiday brochures however which looked very pretty and was only 90 minutes drive from Geneva airport – it was called Châtel in the alpine province of Haute Savoie. Even in June the area was stunning. Although surrounded by wooded slopes and therefore not as high as some of the purpose built resorts because of its northerly latitude, Châtel is colder in winter and keeps its snow well.

Mum and I had a wander round the little town with its funny maze of streets, found a hotel for the night then went to explore; the magic of the place took hold in just the short period and we were hooked. Now for the estate agents. It was quite a buzz looking round estate agents' windows in town knowing that I was looking to sign up to buy a property. When we are on holiday, we all do estate agent window shopping don't we? But the difference is that here I wasn't just looking, I was actually going to *buy a property in a foreign country* – how scary was that?! The majority of properties for sale were apartments, although to be fair there wasn't much choice here. There was the occasional chalet and a few large rundown farmhouses which needed completely rebuilding, but I wasn't up for that.

In one estate agent's office we stopped for a chat (in pigeon French) with a nice chap called Joel. He was very helpful and took time to show us round a couple of apartments, but they were tired, required redecorating and had lousy views up the hill, rather than down into the valley. We needed to see something better than this. In his office he had big plans on the wall for a new development of ski chalets, still to be built. He explained that they had already built a showhouse and he offered to guide us round the site. We got into Joel's car and he started off down the valley. It was only a five minute drive, but it was certainly memorable, mainly because of the speeds we reached. I was in the back and mum sat in the front. I could see she was tensing up as Joel launched us towards each bend on the mountain road, but he seemed oblivious and was happily chatting away about the area and the chalet development. Of course being stiff upper lip 'British', we did not even mention how frightening the ride had been.

Mum in an Alpine meadow – Spring '89 & Max's JCB

When we stopped with relief at the roadside, it was adjacent to a large rectangular concrete block of foundation work – THIS was the showhouse? Perhaps it was lost in translation, but what Joel meant to say or we should have understood, was that the developer had built the *foundations* of the showhouse, but not the actual house itself... At this time we had not met Max the builder by then, maybe if we had, they might have lost a sale... With the guidance of Joel, we toured the site, but apart from the foundations next to the road there was little to see. It was simply a beautiful alpine meadow full of wild flowers in a profusion of colours. The scene was marred only slightly by Max's special two-tone coloured JCB digger - the two colours were yellow and rust!

There were some pegs in the ground and we could see where they were going to lay the footings of the rest of the chalets and we could imagine the views from the house – there would be a different mountain visible from every window. It was midday and quite hot, only one question now, where to go for lunch? I don't know whether Joel recommended it, or perhaps we found it by accident, but we had lunch at the 'Les Cornettes' hotel in the next village down the valley called La Chapelle d'Abondance.

It was definitely the most gorgeous meal in a truly beautiful setting. We had a table to ourselves in the main dining room and marvelled at the huge wood panelled ceiling. Although it was the off-season, all the tables were set for lunch and very proper it was too. Not only that, but all the crockery and glassware were monogrammed with the hotel's name – very nice. We discovered later that we had completely by chance walked into one of the best restaurants on the planet, even though the prices were all very reasonable. Mum was living and working in London at that time and she was used to paying the prices which establishments in the capital can charge. By comparison, Les Cornettes' menu was excellent value for money. We even had the world famous 'salade des Cornettes' as a side dish and were in heaven.

By the time we returned to the estate agent up in Châtel, my mind was made up. This was the place. I agreed the price and signed up the provisional documents and made plans to obtain a mortgage in French Francs, this was completed in Annemasse close to Geneva some weeks later. Joel assured me that the chalets would all be completed in "the spring of 1990" and because I still had not met Max by then, I believed what he said...

*

Whenever I think of Max Bochaton I always smile. Max was the developer, whose small building company constructed the Ski Chalets in the tiny hamlet of L'Hameau du Saix. He was an incorrigible rogue. In many ways he was like a cartoon character and was well known to all who lived in the valley. He was invariably to be seen in his scruffs, with a big bushy beard and long hair, this was the biggest project he had taken on in his life. Imagine one of the larger than life cartoon characters out of 'Asterix the Gaul' and you can picture Max straight away. He was aged in his mid forties back then with the remains of a manly physique that had now been compromised by a substantial beer belly.

This was the house that Max built.

"But Max – you said it would be finished WEEKS AGO...!?"

That being said he was still physically very strong and not averse to showing the workers on the building site how to do things. He was very funny and always game for a laugh however, which perhaps was his downfall in lots of ways, because his humour would often get in the way of the work. Maybe this was one of the reasons why everything took so much longer than it should have done and the timeline for building the chalets overran by a huge amount. In my case, I was not that concerned because I could see that they were actually going to be built eventually - fortunately I had somewhere else to live. Even when the 15 or so chalets had been constructed, the road had not been completed and was still just a rough track until after his death.

That of course was the saddest time - when he died. Over the years that I had known him, I had grown very fond of Max and it was a real shock to the system when I was told he had died. With Max though, his was never likely to be a peaceful end and was probably going to be quite sudden. Of course everybody knew him. He used to laugh when he told us stories about when he was stopped in his car on the mountain road at night by the local Gendarmes of the valley. When they realised he had consumed vast quantities of alcohol, they were at pains to tell him, "S'il vous plait Max! You must drive SLOWLY down the mountain, *you are VERY DRUNK!"*

I recall on several occasions being given a lift by him, once all the way to Geneva airport at 5am. At that time he was driving a black, beaten-up fuel injected VW Jetta which had very clanky front wheel drive. Max explained that the clanking noise was from the Universal Joints which had worn out through wheels spinning on the icy roads in the winter – very reassuring. It sounded initially like he had left the snowchains on! Of course he drove down the mountain road like a lunatic towards the town of Thonon on the edge of Lac Leman; there we turned left for the headlong rush along Lake Geneva's southern shore towards the sleeping Swiss city. I think we made it to Geneva Airport main terminal in slightly under one hour – my best time driving a car had been one hour ten, but Max didn't seem to notice that it was drizzling and that there had been several rockfalls on the mountain road, while thrashing through the gears and smoking a Gauloise!

His surname was Bochaton, "Zees means Pussycat en Anglais" and when he first introduced himself, it was clear that his English was actually quite good; certainly better than my French. His eyes twinkled when he told me that he had lived and worked en Grande Bretagne many years before, which of course accounted for his fluency. He said that he had gone originally to work in the North Sea on the oil rigs and at that time knew very little English. Mischievously he recounted how the first English phrase he had learned was "Zat is NOT my JOB!" A reflection on the "Breeteesh" work ethic, which was why he reckoned the UK was going to hell in a handcart. Perhaps on reflection he was right.

The French Navy and the Royal Navy were often in wars together, but usually not on the same side...

Later on, after I had furnished Chalet Louis and he called round "pour un petit boisson" to see the finished house, I teased him when I showed him an oil painting of a scene from Nelson's time. This depicted a French Navy Frigate striking her colours after being broadsided into submission by a ship of HM Royal Navy and I emphasised that I had been a serving Naval Officer, although we two nations were now allies in NATO of course. He did enjoy a drink though and even in the morning on the building site when I was there finishing the fittings in the house, he was not often without a bottle of Kronenbourg while chatting to his workers.

Of course, it was not all plain sailing either. I remember arriving at Chalet Louis in the very early hours of a Saturday morning having driven all the way from the UK to find that my key did not fit the lock of the front door. Funny, why is that? How can this be? It looked exactly the same as it had done the last time I was there, but quite plainly it did not work, I tried for ages. Time to go and find Max. So at 3 am, I was hammering on the door of his apartment up in the village of Châtel and it took ages for him to answer. When he came to the door however and saw me looking puzzled and vexed holding the front door key to Chalet Louis, realisation dawned across his face, he said, "Ah! Errrr...we *CHANGE* zee lock... *Dernier semaine,* erm... last er, week it was and 'ere is zee new key, I so sorry, *Je regret* James!"

Well you could never be angry with him for very long and there was a perfectly reasonable explanation – when they had lost the key and could not get in to carry out some finishing works, they simply drilled the lock out and fitted a new one. No thought of course to call me in the UK and warn me for the next time I came - which would have prevented me from having all those spare keys cut which were now worthless...

He had been many things in his lifetime and it was not always easy to separate the fact from the fiction. He had at various times been an oil rig contractor, a Paris-Dakar rally driver, a ski instructor, an hotelier owning one of the small hotels up in Châtel village and now he was a property developer. Of all the things which he was good at however, his most accomplished role was Bon Viveur! He really did live life at 200 kilometres per hour and was renowned throughout the valley. Infamous and notorious probably sum up the ways in which the locals all knew him; but that being said he was such a character that nobody seemed to mind. If he promised faithfully to do a job for you, then he would get around to it eventually.

I had reason to be grateful to him on more than one occasion, for example when I rather stupidly left Chalet Louis in the first winter to return to the UK and switched off everything. No I really mean EVERYTHING! All the water and all of the electricity, which meant that the predictable occurred as the temperature fell to minus 26 degrees Celsius in the following week and stayed there for days... The pipes froze and burst - even the water in the toilet bowl froze and smashed the porcelain. Then when it thawed, there was the predictable flood. Upon my arrival a few weeks later, I realised the foolishness of what I had done and called Max for help. He didn't even flinch and just got his boys to come and sort it all out for me – there was no charge! *"Haute service!"* as they say over there.

Naturally it worked both ways of course, as the next summer I arrived unannounced to find that Chalet Louis had been opened up and that one of Max's merry men had attached a thick electrical cable to my mains electric fuse board which was routed out of the window and across the site to power some of their equipment. I got a large screwdriver out and unscrewed the cable from my mains supply and threw the offending wire out of the window. No wonder my electric bills were inexplicably high?! According to my girlfriend Gill, I had a face like thunder during the disconnection process, but by the time I saw Max again I had calmed down and just asked him to make sure they asked in future.

Months behind schedule, Chalet Louis takes shape

Winter 1989

Gill and I had actually arrived from the South of France on a motorcycle, much to Max's amusement when he saw it. Oh yes, he would love motorcycles wouldn't he? We had ridden down from the UK through France the previous week to see the 24 hour motorcycle endurance race called Le Bol d'Or at the Paul Ricard (Le Castellet) circuit near Toulon. After the frenetic pace of the weekend at the track, we had then chilled out by spending some time cruising and camping along the French Riviera until it had been time to head for the Alps. That ride from the south coast of France, all the way to Chalet Louis was a bucket-list experience and it was with an amazing tingly "we're coming home" feeling that we rode over the pass from Switzerland into the top end of Le Vallee d'Abondance – gorgeous.

From the Côte d'Azur to the French Alps Sept '92

The next morning, Gill and I took the 'bike up into Châtel to get some bits and pieces from the supermarket and the hardware shop. Just outside le supermarché in our leathers we bumped into Max – big hugs and kisses all round. We told him we had arrived from the Riviera and he was delighted – "Zees calls pour un petit Boisson!" he said, leading us by the hand through the door of the large builder's merchants. There we were introduced to Geo (pronounced Joe), the owner who later became one of our neighbours in the valley, just over the road from Chalet Louis. We all went into the back office behind the counter and a bottle of Pastis was produced with some little glasses and a small jug of water. He giggled as we told him all about our travels on the motorbike through France and he was genuinely pleased that we had made such a journey to end up at my house in the valley. The holiday was a great success of course and the valley got even further under our skin – this was the summer of 1992.

During the winters of the next few years, we got ourselves organised such that we could enjoy truly memorable skiing holidays with our family and friends. At the same time we rented out the weeks we could not use ourselves. We became quite adept at self-catering skiing holidays and often found ourselves cooking for large numbers of friends and family. As you can imagine, we were not the only ones cooking, if there was a large group of us in residence, then we established a cooking Rota whereby everybody took it in turns to cook – many of the recipes come from these times when our friends gave us their "signature dishes" to try. Before a few years had gone by, the Chalet Louis Cookbook was burgeoning with great food and drink combinations.

I recall one particular week when we had 14 adults and 2 babies in Chalet Louis – and everyone had a bed to sleep in! Every night dinner was prepared by teams of two chefs and it is fair to say we all ate very well that week.

"Where DID we park the bus last night...?

During these self-catering years, we did spend a lot of time sampling the food and wines of the local restaurants. We justified this by saying that we were sometimes forced to eat out in order to provide a comprehensive guide for future chalet guests. The bars of Châtel also received our attention of course and many were the times that we spent happy evenings in the company of friends in places like Bar L'Isba, which was also the local pub for Max. The reason for this was more than just sociable, but also geographical as Bar L'Isba was on the ground floor of the apartment block where Max lived. In the early nineties, this bar was one of the most happening places in the village and you could always guarantee a cheerful evening with a warm welcome from both friends and strangers alike.

We had a brilliant Hi-Fi system in the Ski Chalet and this added to the fact that there were no close neighbours to complain about the noise, resulted in many a musical evening. As you can see, music leads to dancing...

Chalet Louis – "dance in France" evening - mid '90s

Après-ski children's entertainment – early '00s

I remember in the days before the Euro when French Francs were the currency. We had only a few Francs in our pockets as we were departing next morning back to the UK. Gill and I decided that we ought to pop in "for just one drink" to say goodbye. Well, at closing time we rolled out of the place, having enjoyed a most hospitable evening with some extremely friendly and generous folk, having consumed plenty of team spirit – we still had our few French Francs untouched. As Paul Daniels would have said, "now THAT'S magic!"

By 1994 Gill and I were married and had another house to decorate and furnish back in the UK, which limited our time in Châtel that summer. On a sunny afternoon in August, only a week before we were due to fly out to France again, I arrived home to the worst news – "Max.. He's DEAD!" I shook my head in disbelief and went outside. I sat down in the sun in the back garden – tears came easily. It hurt so much and I cried and cried – it was such a shock. Perhaps the worst thing was that he died in an aircraft accident when the light aircraft in which he was a passenger, suffered an engine failure. They were near Aosta in the Alps at the time and if you know that area, you can imagine the difficulties of carrying out a successful forced landing there – virtually impossible.

The details emerged later. The single-engined aeroplane had been hired by Max and his Architect for a pleasure flight over the Alps and all six seats were full. Unable to restart the failed engine, they hit the ground too hard and the aircraft broke up on impact - there was a fireball. Apparently Max had been sitting on the back row of seats next to the Architect's teenage daughter and the Post Mortem showed that her body was least burned of all. By the position of the corpses, Max had tried to protect her from the effects of the crash. It was entirely in keeping with the nature of the man I knew that he would try to save another's life, even while he was in the process of losing his own...

At his funeral the following week, nearly all the inhabitants of Le Val d'Abondance turned out to mourn his passing – over 1000 people attended. I am sure however that he would not have enjoyed growing old. He had such a love of life that his decline with the passing decades would not have been a graceful affair. Now of course he will never grow old, but will be forever in our memories at the age of fifty. He was the life and soul of any gathering. He enriched the lives of the people he touched, even though some of them did not know it at the time. It took his death to make that realisation occur.

In 1996 while flying Boeing 767s as a Captain for Alitalia on the contract based in Milan, we often used to pass the airways waypoint of Aosta in the climb out of Malpensa heading for New York. I often looked down into those steep sided valleys from the flightdeck of the airliner and wonder what would have become of him had the engine not quit...

Max was survived by his widow Genevieve and their young son. Genevieve was concerned that Max's work was finished properly and she was the one who released the money from his estate and authorised the building of the road outside Chalet Louis. For this we chalet owners were all very grateful. It could have ended differently had she not decided to tie up all the loose ends.

His legacy however was a development of beautiful wooden houses built with steeply pitched roofs and overhanging eaves that are a joy to inhabit either in winter or summer. The double thickness walls are well insulated against the extreme temperatures which can occur in the French Alps and the inside of the chalets are warm and cosy. They are an ideal venue for après-ski activities, not least of which is the evening meal – which is primarily what this book is all about.

Breakfasts are often quite a hurried affair as there is always an urgency to get out of the house in time for ski-lessons, to be first in the queue for the lifts or to get a good space in the car park. Lunch is either taken in a mountain restaurant or café, which may be expensive or eaten as a packed lunch and we have some suggestions for those too. The main thrust of the book is to give guidance for the evening meal, which is the main gourmet event of the day on a skiing holiday.

BaBeth's Place for lunch - Plaine Dranse

Our tried and tested recipes gained over twenty years of self-catering skiing holidays with family and friends in the Alps, have been divided into three colours – we've called them pistes. Just as the slopes are colour coded, the same goes for our recipes, the easiest being green, then for intermediates come the blue runs and finally the red.

Experienced skiing-chefs may well be asking why we have not put in a 'black piste' section and our answer to that is we assumed you didn't want to burn anything... A word of reassurance – just because there are recipes (blues and reds) which are slightly more complicated to prepare, please don't let this put you off. In a similar way to obtaining great satisfaction from skiing the blue and red runs as we progress through our skiing and boarding – the same can be said of these slightly more advanced food preparation areas.

Steak Fondue Chalet Louis style and...

...the ideal way to work up an appetite

A common theme throughout this book is that none of the recipes are difficult – that's the whole point of course. If you have opted for a self-catering skiing holiday, the last thing you need is to be a constant slave in the kitchen. As we have indicated elsewhere in the text, the fact that you are self-catering, means that you will save hundreds of pounds in feeding your ski party. This cookbook will earn its keep for you many times over.

James McBride

08 SEP 2015

Chalet Louis 1990

Yes, this really was the house that Max built

2 GREEN PISTE - STARTERS

Camembert Starter   around 15 mins   **Serves 8**

The Backstory

This one really is an old chestnut and so simple – I mean how hard can it be, to take the top off the Camembert box and put the cheese in the oven? Guaranteed results every time. If we had a 'Nursery Slope' section this one would be top of the list. Thanks to our friend Susan Gordon Tait for this one – she really is so *cultured*, it's hard to believe she's an Australian…!

The Gear

- Okay, so you will have to go and buy a large Camembert cheese
- 1 large clove of peeled, crushed garlic – this is the hardest part I think

- Half a glass or less, of dry white wine – choose it carefully and share the rest of the bottle with the assistant chefs!

The Way

Well, we've nearly told you how to do it above, but if you really need instructions, here goes;

- Preheat the oven to 190 degrees Celsius – technical eh?
- Take the top off the cheese box – tricky manoeuvre this one, don't fall over
- Now remove the cheese from its plastic wrapper and replace back into the box
- Make some criss-cross cuts in the top of the cheese - fill these with crushed garlic
- Dribble white wine (yes... you've dribbled white wine before) into the garlicky cuts
- Wrap in aluminium foil and bake in the oven for 25 mins
- Serve hot to the table for people to scoop out onto French bread – yummy!

Chicken/Veggie Wraps   50 mins   Serves 8

The Backstory

In April 2006, we had lunch in a restaurant overlooking the pyramids in Cairo. We enjoyed these chicken and veggie wraps so much we had to get the recipe from the chef. Thanks Mustafa.

The Gear

- 6 boneless chicken breast fillets
- 4 courgettes
- 4 red onions
- 4 red peppers
- 4 yellow peppers
- A handful of fresh basil leaves
- 8 tsp red pesto
- 8 large tortilla wraps
- A little Olive's Oil
- Salt n black pepper to season

The Way

- Preheat the oven to 180 degrees Celsius
- Deseed and slice all the peppers
- Cut courgettes into strips and onions into wedge shapes, place on baking tray
- Sprinkle seasoning and olive oil on them and roast for 25 mins or till tender
- Simultaneously season and cook the chicken in a frying pan, then cut into strips
- Get all the tortillas out and spread each with a tsp of pesto, then layer some of the cooked veggies with the chicken and some fresh basil on each one, roll and cut in half - enjoy

Chicken liver Pâté   10 mins to make (8 hours chillin') Serves 8

The Backstory

Those who like pâté will *love* this recipe. When Jim Gilchrist (famous Al Jazeera news correspondent) came skiing with us, we nearly bought all of the duck pâté in the northern French Alps – or so it seemed.

The Gear

- 50g butter
- One medium white onion
- One clove garlic crushed
- One bay leaf
- One pinch thyme
- 225g chicken livers
- Salt and black pepper
- 2 tablespoons brandy

The Way

- Melt butter, fry onions, bay leaf n thyme for 2-3 mins
- Cut livers into small pieces and add to pan
- Fry gently for 6-7 mins
- Remove bay leaf
- Blend mixture with hand blender or if one not available force through a sieve until smooth add brandy n salt & pepper to taste.
- Pour mixture into a serving dish and chill overnight – 8 hours+

Serve as a starter, with crusty bread or hot toast

***

Salads, Soups 'n Snacks

Best Rice Salad on the Planet   15-20 mins   **Serves 6**

The Backstory

This one came originally from our good mate Amanda, the *"taxi driver's friend…"* Actually, that bit's not true, because Amanda used to have some major ding-dongs with them late at night when they were trying to get her in the cab to go home, but THAT is another story ☺ She was the life and soul of the party and we sorely miss her. No don't worry, she didn't die; she just moved away with her family down south! She's a lovely creative person who missed her vocation as a singer. If there had been an X-Factor competition twenty years ago, she would have won it.

The Gear

- 100 g long grain rice
- 150 mls oil and vinegar dressing (separate recipe below)
- 1 medium sized green pepper
- 1 bunch spring onions
- 2 tbsp seedless raisins
- 50g flaked almonds
- 1 peeled peach, chopped up – no, seriously! Amanda said so.

The Way

- Cook the rice in boiling salted water for about 8 to 10 mins until just tender
- Drain well & turn into a mixing bowl add 2-3 tablespoons of oil and vinegar dressing, toss to coat the rice and set aside until completely cool - or Phat if you're a boarder!
- Halve, deseed & finely chop the green pepper, trim and finely chop the spring onions

- Add pepper & spring onions to the rice with the raisins and the remaining dressing
- Toss altogether, then just before serving grill the flaked almonds until golden brown and sprinkle with salt – stir into the rice salad with the chopped, peeled peach

The Oil & Vinegar dressing

- Dash of French mustard
- 1 tbsp white wine vinegar
- Salt and pepper
- 3 tbsps of oil
- 1 tsp balsamic vinegar

Mix the mustard and a good seasoning of salt and pepper with a fork until blended. Add the oil and beat vigorously until an emulsion is formed. Note that the oil separates –so beat it again before using.

***

"Swiss Miss" Wurstsalat　　　**10 mins tops**　　　**Serves 4**

The Backstory

This is perfect to pack in a Tupperware dish in the rucksack together with a baguette for an eat anytime snack or a light lunch. Great for the slopes (make sure that lid is tightly closed on the Tupperware dish!!!)

The Gear

- Four hard boiled eggs shelled and cut into quarters
- Two Gherkins sliced into eighths
- Chives
- Four Radishes thinly sliced
- 250g sliced and diced Emmental cheese
- 500g of precooked sausage skinned and sliced thinly
- (Cervelat or Fleishwurst are ideal)
- Five tablespoons olive oil or sunflower oil
- Four tablespoons white wine vinegar

- One teaspoon mayonnaise
- One clove garlic pressed or very finely chopped
- Salt and black pepper

The Way

- Prepare salad sauce by putting oil, vinegar, mayonnaise, garlic into a sealable jar (we usually use an old jam jar) and shake ingredients to mix and season with salt and pepper.
- In a large salad bowl toss radishes, cheese and sausage together
- Just before serving shake the salad sauce again (the oil and vinegar can separate if stood too long)and mix into the salad
- Garnish with the quartered eggs, gherkins and a few chopped chives

"Swiss Miss" Wurtsalat

Berni Chetham

***

Châtel Croque Monsieur   10 minutes   Serves 2

The Backstory

A snack that is good to eat at any time. Our good friend "Crock" in Châtel was one of the very first non-French Pisteurs in the French Alps and we were very proud of him.

The Gear

- Four slices white bread
- Dijon mustard
- 125g Groviera or Gruyere cheese sliced
- Four slices ham
- Butter

The Way

- Spread each slice of bread with butter on both sides.
- Spread Dijon mustard on two of the slices of bread on one side only
- Place a slice of ham on the each of the slices with mustard and slices of cheese on the other.
- Sandwich together
- Heat a little butter in a frying pan and fry the sandwiches or 2-3 minutes each side until golden and the cheese melted
- Slice in half and serve immediately.

In Crock's Avalanche Bar in Châtel

"Cross-Rocket" Salad   about 3 mins   Serves 8

The Way

Wash a large bag of rocket leaves and put even amounts into 8 bowls. Chop up 8 tomatoes with 4 or 5 banana shallots – mix altogether in a large bowl, then add to the little bowls.

Use balsamic vinegar dressing and some fresh ground black pepper on top of each one.

Job done. Goes well with pasta dishes.

***

Tomato & Mozarella Tart   25 minutes   Serves 6

The Backstory

A nice easy one this. It makes either a great starter or a snack. Based upon the old Italian Tricolore Salad idea of tomato, mozzarella cheese and basil (red, white and green). It takes literally 5 minutes to knock up, then 20 minutes in a preheated oven.

The Gear

- Two or three large tomatoes thinly sliced
- Hunk of mozzarella cheese (Buffalo if you like)
- Large sheet of ready made puff pastry
- 1 tbsp Pesto sauce
- Sprinkling of Black Pepper
- Fresh Basil leaves to garnish (Coriander works too)

The Way

Roll out the pastry evenly on a large baking tray and double it over at the edges all the way round. Then cover the sheet with pesto all the way to the sides. Now layer the pastry with the tomato slices.

Sprinkle the whole with fresh ground black pepper according to taste, then add the cut up pieces of mozzarella.

Put the tray in a preheated oven at 190 degrees Celsius for 20 minutes or until the cheese has melted and browned on the top.

Add the fresh Basil leaves decoratively **after** it comes out of the oven.

Two large trays – serves 12 as a starter

Tomato and Mozarella Tart – with fresh Basil

***

Engelberg Onion Soup　　　　**45 minutes**　　　　**Serves 4**

The Backstory

A great energy boost for lunch or perfect as a starter, this stuff really does warm the cockles!!! I know it's a strange name (Engelberg) and those of us of a certain age, have the urge to shout……. Humperdink!

The Gear

- Two tablespoons butter
- Four medium white onions peeled and thinly sliced and chopped
- One clove garlic finely chopped
- One medium glass (150ml) red wine

- One tablespoon brandy
- 700ml high quality beef broth (or if you must 3 beef stock cubes in boiling water)
- Dash of Worcester sauce if you have some or a dash of balsamic vinegar
- Gruyere
- Baguette
- Salt and freshly ground black pepper to taste

The Way

- Warm butter in a frying pan
- Fry the onions until soft and slightly golden season with salt and pepper
- Transfer onions to a large sauce pan and with the exception of the cheese and baguette add the remaining ingredients
- Stir and simmer for 30 minutes add extra pepper/salt as required
- Lightly toast two slices of baguette per soup bowl under a grill
- Top each slice with a piece of gruyere and grill until bubbling
- Serve the soup with 2 slices of cheesy baguette floating on the top

***

Tell's Tomato Surprise!   **35 mins**   **Serves 6**

The Backstory

Quick, simple and delicious. We thought this one originated from Berni's Uncle Tell... but then she told us she didn't HAVE an uncle Tell... Whatever; it's a good one, thanks Tell whoever you are!

The Gear

- Six beef tomatoes
- Six 1cm deep slices of baguette toasted
- 180g goats cheese rind removed and crumbled
- 150g mozzarella chopped into small cubes
- Two tablespoon chopped basil
- Two tablespoons chopped walnuts
- Salt and freshly ground black pepper
- Olive oil

The Way

- Pre heat oven to 190°C
- Slice a very thin slice from the bottom of each tomato to help them stand up straight
- Cut the top of each tomato and keep to one side
- Then using a teaspoon remove the seeds and pulp from each tomato
- In a bowl mix the mozzarella, walnuts, goats' cheese and basil season with salt and pepper.
- Stuff each tomato with the mixture make sure each tomato has at least 3 cubes of mozzarella
- Place each tomato on a toasted piece of baguette
- Cook in the oven for 15 minutes until the cheese looks melted and golden
- Serve with the tomato top lids placed back on and a little drizzle of olive oil

Tell's Tomato Surprise

The Backstory

This reminds me of the complaint letter which we received in the easyJet office in Liverpool years ago. A little old lady on one of our Geneva flights complained that the rough handling by the security guard at the x-ray meant that a paper bag got squashed and "the French tarts were spoiled..." In the office we reckoned that *all the French tarts in Geneva were spoilt* – "Mais, c'est normale madame!"

The Gear

- A pack of Filo pastry, easy! Comes in 400g packs but you will use only some of this.
- 50g butter
- 750g onions, sliced
- 3 egg yolks
- 250ml double cream
- Salt and pepper
- grated nutmeg

The Way

- Grease a 20cm flan tin or other open dish and line with the pastry.
- Melt the butter in a pan add the onions and fry gently for about 25 minutes until golden brown. Leave to cool. Beat the egg yolks and cream. Add salt pepper and nutmeg as you wish. Add the onions and mix well.
- Put this into the pastry lined dish. Bake in preheated oven 200 deg Celsius for 30 minutes or until pastry golden brown. Serve hot.

***

3 GREEN PISTE – MAINS

Shredders Tuna Pasta with Cheese   **35 mins tops   Serves 8**

The Backstory

Yes we know you're a long way from the sea, but eating seafood pasta in the mountains has a touch of the exotic about it – we hope you'll agree. Also tuna is full of protein, v. healthy!

Shredders Tuna Pasta with Cheese

The Gear

- 160g firm cheese grated (cheddar is good)
- 400g tinned, drained sweetcorn (a large tin)
- 360g Tuna chunks, flaked (a large tin)
- 330g Pasta (any shape)
- One sliced red pepper
- Large tin of tomatoes
- A few chopped mushrooms

White Sauce

- 60g butter

- 60g plain flour
- 500ml milk

The Way

- Preheat oven to 180C (gas mark 4)
- Cook Pasta like it says on the packet, then drain it
- White Sauce – make with butter, plain flour & 500 ml Milk. Add ¾ of the cheese to the sauce – try to be smooth….
- Place pasta in a large, deep ovenproof dish, add the tuna, sweetcorn, vegetables and cheese sauce & mix it all up
- Evenly apply the remainder of the grated cheese on the top
- Cook in the oven for 15 minutes or until all the cheese has melted
- It goes down really well with a salad side dish!

***

"Sandra" Chilly Con Carne   **45 mins max**   **Serves 8**

The Backstory

Chilly? Well we went skiing to the French Alps a few winters back and it was -26°C at nights and that was waaaayyyy too chilly for us. In fact it was too cold for the brand new hirecar which wouldn't even start until we had pushed it into the garage at the ski chalet to warm it up to only minus 8 degrees! Literally there was just a 'click' from the starter motor solenoid and nothing else when we turned the key – *"Ahh they don't make 'em like they used to. Now if that had been my old Series 3 Land Rover called Sandra…. she always started, however cold it was"* Anyway here's the answer to chilliness, a lovely Con Carne – best served hot of course.

The Gear

- 500g *lean* mince (lean on the outside ski…☺)
- Couple of finely chopped carrots, chop, chop, chop
- Chilli Powder – one level teaspoon is mild - suggest less for the kids
- Tin of baked beans
- Tin of kidney beans
- Splash of Olive's Oil
- Couple of small onions – more fine chopping required
- Couple of tins of tomatoes (chop me Charlie!)

- Couple of Garlic cloves (crush 'em baby!)
- Small tin of sweetcorn (rinse me honey!)

The Way

- Large casserole dish, heat it up with the splash of Olive's Oil on the bottom
- Cook the onions gently for 5 mins until they are soft, soft, soft
- In goes the mince and cook it through, stirring the while – brown it off
- Now add the kidney beans 'n sweetcorn to the mix
- Stir in the chopped Toms, bakey beans, crushed garlic and carry-rots
- Simmer gently for 30 mins with an occasional stir (act casual here)
- Ideal served with Rice for the big kids – for the little ones, try them with mini Pitta pockets with some grated cheese 'n salad – they like to fill the pockets themselves

***

Pasta lunch in Avoriaz – simple & delicious

Chalet Arthur Chicken   55 mins max   Serves 8

The Backstory

Chalet Arthur is next door to Chalet Louis and we go back there to ski every year in January. We all love this one. It's dead easy to make, the taste is fabulous and it goes really well with baked potatoes and salad. Or alternatively try it with rice or pasta. You're guaranteed to see clean plates here chef! You can substitute Broccoli for Asparagus quite easily.

The Gear

- 8 Chicken breast fillets – cut into 1 inch cubes (that's 2.4 cms BTW)
- 2 Tins condensed mushroom soup – we're not cheating here really
- 200g gr8td cheese – cheddar or similar hard stuff
- Large bunch Asparagus – say 12-15 stalks, chopped into 1" pieces
- 2 tbsp mayonnaise
- 3 tsp curry powder
- 250ml chicken stock
- 1 tbsp olive's oil

White Sauce

- 60g butter
- 60g plain flour
- 500ml milk

The Way

- Brown off the chicken chunks in a frying pan for 5 mins with the oil
- Wash/Trim the asparagus and cut into 1" pieces – add them raw
- Preheat the oven to 160C – medium heat
- White Sauce – make with butter, plain flour & 500 ml Milk. Add the gr8td cheese to the sauce – try to make it smooth, just like your ski instructor ahead of you on the slopes
- In the sauce, add the curry powder, mushroom soup, chicken stock and mayo, stir well

- Mix the chicken, asparagus n' sauce in a large ovenproof dish
- In the oven then for 45 minutes n' make sure chicken is cooked through, no pink bits
- Now… while that's all happening go and have a large glass of wine to celebrate and get your assistant chef to rustle up the salad

Chalet Arthur Chicken with Asparagus…

…and the same dish with Broccoli

Livigno Veggie Lasagne   about 50 mins   Serves 6-8

The Backstory

According to legend, it's not easy to be a true vegetarian while living in France – they do seem to enjoy their meat don't they? Well, here's one for the veggies and very tasty too, even if you like meaty Lasagne. It is best served with a plain green salad, not too much dressing, perhaps just a little Balsamic vinegar – the Lasagne is rich enough.

The Gear

- 1 kilo of sliced vegetables as follows; 1 aubergine, 1 courgette, big handful of mushrooms, 1 yellow and 1 red pepper
- 2 tins chopped tomatoes
- 2 large onions – chopped – one red one, one white one
- 2 cloves garlic – chopped
- Tsp Paprika
- Tbsp Oregano
- A box (about 10 or 12) Dried Pasta Sheets
- Seasoning (fresh ground black pepper and salt to taste)
- 2 Tbsp Olive's Oil
- 200g Grated Cheese (leave a bit to put on the top)

White Sauce

- 60g butter
- 60g plain flour
- 500ml milk

The Way

- Fry the chopped veggies and onions in Olive's Oil for 10 to 12 mins on high heat, stirring all the time
- Then add the toms, paprika, garlic and oregano, bringing to the boil and seasoning with S&P. Preheat the oven to 190 degrees Celsius

- White Sauce – make with butter, plain flour & 500 ml Milk. Add ¾ of the cheese to the sauce – make it as smooth as your last turns on that Blue motorway piste you skied this afternoon!
- Take one large greased ovenproof gratin dish and layer alternately with veggies, sauce and pasta sheets – finish with a top layer of veggies and the remainder of the grated cheese
- Now it's into the oven for 25 or 30 mins until the top is like the old song by 'The Stranglers'...

***

The Fall-Line Fish Dish **around 30 mins** **Serves 8**

The Backstory

Here's a great fish recipe from our friends Jane (oh, she knows EVERYONE in Knutsford ☺) and Chris who live on a farm in Cheshire – yes we know that's a long way from the coast, however, it's easy to make, enjoyed by all and healthy too! Jane and Chris have gone from breeding pigs all the way through to making their own sausages, so they're really living the Good Life now!

The Gear

- 8 fillets of fish – can be Hake, Cod, Haddock, approx 200g per fillet
- 2 lemons
- 4 cloves of garlic
- Salt and pepper to season
- 250 g watercress
- 10 tbsp Olive's Oil
- 2.5 Kg King Edward potatoes – the older tatties are better

The Way

- Peeling potatoes is not everyone's idea of fun, so here's a job you can delegate to the assistant chef. They should be cut into chunks, all about the same size - then rinsed and boiled in salted water. When they are tender, take off the heat and drain
- Preheat oven now to 200 degrees Celsius

- Spread olive oil (2 tbsps) on an oven tray then lay the fillets, skin side down on top
- Lubricate with another 2 tbsps of oil, squeeze over with lemon juice and sprinkle with salt & pepper. Bake in the oven for 10 or 15 mins depending on thickness of the fish and then peel and chop the garlic with some salt, mix to a paste
- Put the garlic and oil in the pan you used for the potatoes, heating for a minute, and then return the hot tatties and watercress to mix them all up. Break up the potatoes, but don't mash 'em
- Drain the juices from the fish into the tatties mix, add salt & pepper then a final stir
- Serve the fish lying on a bed of crushed, mixed potatoes – artistically arranged ☺

***

Carver's Carbonara   **around 15 mins**   **Serves 8**

The Backstory

Could there be an easier dish than Carbonara? And tasty too. This is a light one for maybe a late evening meal when too heavy a dish would not be welcomed, or perhaps you could have this as one course then add a desert. Legend has it that it was invented for Italian charcoal workers and it became known as 'Coal-miners spaghetti' Now it's cool-skiers spaghetti!

The Gear

- Thin Spaghetti
- 4 eggs
- 8 slices of ham
- 4 tbsps crème fraiche
- 1 tbsp chopped parsley
- Fresh ground black pepper
- 2 tbsp Olive's Oil

The Way

- Boil the spaghetti in salted water
- Dice the ham and chop the parsley
- Into a bowl add the eggs and crème fraiche – whisk together
- When the spaghetti is ready, drain and place in the pan with the ham, stir in olive oil
- Now add the egg mixture and mix thoroughly, add the parsley & black pepper
- If it looks a bit dry – just add a little more olive oil

***

Cruisin' Thai Green Curry   **around 25 mins**   **Serves 8**

The Backstory

A really tasty curry this one and very popular, even with those who say they don't like curry. Based on an old Thai recipe, we have our Hannah to thank for this one, she found it and made it for us all the first time, and yes we raved about it – Hurrah for HanHan! It is so ridiculously easy, when you are in the kitchen, you are going to have to *pretend* it's more complicated!

The Gear

- 1 bunch spring onions
- 2 cloves garlic – peeled n crushed
- 200g green beans
- 8 chicken breast fillets
- The juice of one fresh lime
- 400g (a large) tin of coconut milk
- 1 ½ tbsp green Thai curry paste
- 20g fresh coriander

The Way

- Top n tail the green beans
- Cut chicken into small chunks
- Fry the spring onions, crushed garlic & chicken in oil for 3 or 4 mins

- Stir in green curry paste and green beans
- Add the coconut milk and simmer for 15 mins
- Squeeze out lime
- Chuck in the coriander – then you're done hun!
- Served with rice is nice ☺

***

Ashley's Vegetarian Moussaka   about 50 mins   Serves 6

The Backstory

There are always a variety of tinned beans available abroad, more so than in the UK. It really does not matter which you choose. Haricot, broad, butter, cannelloni etc. Any will do for this. Ashley is what you call a lifelong friend, even though he's a stout vegetarian. Back in '95 he spent a lot of time with us at Chalet Louis while we did some woodwork together – his DIY skills are legendary and he's also a mean cook.

The Gear

- 2 Aubergines, sliced into 1 cm slices
- Oil of any type
- 3 cloves garlic, finely chopped
- 2 onions, chopped
- 1 leek, sliced.   Or celery if leek unavailable
- 2 peppers, any colour, chopped
- 400g tin of tomatoes, preferably plum tomatoes
- 300g tinned beans. See above guide to the tinned beans of Europe
- About half a big tub of plain yogurt, or two small tubs
- 1 egg
- 100g cheese, grated

The Way

- Preheat the oven to 180 degrees
- Fry the onion, leek and garlic for 5 minutes in a saucepan.

- Add the beans, peppers and tomatoes. Break up the tomatoes. Let it bubble away for 10 minutes.
- Meanwhile fry the aubergine slices for a few minutes on both sides.
- In a casserole dish place a layer of the aubergine slices then a layer of sauce. Then the rest of the aubergines and the rest of the sauce.
- Mix yogurt, egg and half the grated cheese and pour it on top. Then sprinkle the remaining cheese on that.
- Place in oven for 35 minutes

***

Traditional Berthoud   **20 mins**   **Serves 4**

The Backstory

Made with Abondance cheese which is a great example of a gourmet mountain cheese with origins that date back some 700 years. It is a semi hard cheese with a fruity flavour. Berthoud is a really traditional French Alpine recipe from the Savoie and Haute Savoie regions, but dead easy to make.

The Gear

- 800g of Abondance cheese
- 8 potatoes – washed with skins left on
- 1 clove garlic
- Salt and pepper to season
- ½ litre of Apremont, white wine (any dry white will do really)

The Way

- Preheat the oven to 210 degrees Celsius
- Boil the potatoes – then simmer for 15 or 20 mins until cooked
- While the potatoes are cooking, cut the cheese into very thin slices
- Peel the garlic and rub it around the inside of four little ovenproof shallow bowls
- Put equal portions of cheese into each bowl then add the wine in equal amounts
- Add the salt and pepper

- Into the oven now for 10 mins – the top should be golden brown and bubbling
- Serve hot with the potatoes and a little plain salad
- Best wine with this dish is Crépy, Apremont or Ripaille from Haute Savoie

***

Booter Baked Chicken	**50 mins**	**Serves 8**

The Backstory

Everybody loves the chicken, especially when baked and served in a meal like this one. You will achieve super-chef status with this one – never fails to please.

The Gear

- 8 boneless chicken breasts
- 6 sticks of celery – thin sliced
- 6 tbsp Greek yoghurt or double cream
- 10 tbsp chicken stock
- 100g grated cheese
- 2 tins condensed chicken soup
- 2 onions – chopped fine
- 2 green peppers – deseeded and chopped fine
- 2 tbsp dried parsley
- 4 bags of cheese and onion crisps
- 5 tbsp Olive's Oil
- Salt and pepper

The Way

- Preheat the oven to 190 degrees Celsius
- Skin off the breasts, then cut the chicken into 1 inch (2.4cm) cubes
- Brown the chicken off in a frying pan with the oil for about 5 mins, until just cooked
- Remove the chicken to a large bowl
- Now add a splash more oil if required. Fry onion, peppers and celery until tender – not brown

- Pour this mixture over the chicken, then stir in the soup, yoghurt, stock, parsley & seasoning
- Give it all a good stir and place in a large ovenproof dish
- Sprinkle the cheese over the top and add crushed crisps
- Bakey, bakey in the middle of the oven for 35 mins

***

Raclette   **15 mins for tatties**   **Serves various**

The Backstory

Now here's a meal that everybody cooks for themselves at the table – trust the French to think of that. Mind you they have spent several hundred years producing the best cheeses for this sort of thing. It's a great way to have a meal together with family and friends – in fact we have one back home in the UK from time to time during the winter. Similar to fondue, I suppose it's a bit of a cheat putting this in as a 'recipe', but many people don't know what it is. I always think of our good friend Steve Kadera when we have Raclette, because he can shift half a metric tonne of cheese at one sitting! Hahaha! (Mind you he is a Triathlete, so we'll forgive him).

The Gear

- You will need a raclette grill – nothing special here, but a tabletop one is fine
- Raclette cheese sliced into squares about 8cm x 8cms and fairly thin – in France of course you can buy it off the shelf, in the UK you can ask for it at the cheese counter, they may even slice it for you if asked nicely. Raclette cheese is unpasteurised
- Small bowl of silverskin onions
- Small bowl of mini-gherkins
- Large bowl of small sized new potatoes, boiled with their skins on - French style
- Platter of cold meats (Charcuterie as the French say) including parma ham, salami sausage slices and a few other sliced sausage meats

- Maggi sauce – for seasoning
- Aromat

The Way

- Most common tabletop raclette cookers have little metal spatula style dishes in which to cook the cheese – each guest puts theirs under the grill & when the cheese bubbles, it's done!
- In the meantime, everyone puts the potatoes onto their plates, open them up and season with the maggi, aromat, salt and pepper
- Add the cold meats on the side, with the onions and gherkins
- When the cheese is cooked, remove from the grill and scrape off with a wooden spatula onto the potato/plate – bon appetit!

Traditional Raclette – French Alps style

Sausage Casserole   10mins prep/30 mins cook   Serves 8

The Backstory

Wherever you travel, the humble banger will always be available. This is especially true in Europe of course, where each nation seems to pride itself on producing wonderful sausage creations. Using good quality sausages is money well spent here as they are the mainstay. Best served with mashed potato of course.

The Gear

- 1 kilo of sausages
- 200g bacon – chopped up
- 2 onions – finally chopped
- 1 large tin sweet corn
- 1 large tin kidney beans
- 2 x 400g tins of tomatoes
- 2 tbsp tomato puree
- 2 red peppers – deseeded and finally chopped
- 2 tsp Thyme
- 1 tbsp Olive's Oil
- Freshly ground black pepper

The Way

- Grill the sausages until brown all over
- Simultaneously fry the bacon and onion together in a big casserole dish in the oil
- Into the casserole put the sausages, kidney beans, sweet corn, tomatoes & pepper
- Add thyme seasoning and some freshly ground black pepper
- Now, in goes the tomato puree and some boiling water, if it's looking dry
- Cover and simmer for 20 mins

***

Linguine Carbonara á la Ghidouche   25 mins   Serves 8

The Backstory

This recipe of Sarah's, is quick and easy to make and tastes delicious. For the pasta you can use either spaghetti or linguine, but we have found that whereas with spaghetti you're looking forward to the next mouthful, with linguine you just can't wait! If you have kids who don't like mushrooms you can cook them separately.

The Gear

- Linguine Pasta (standard pack, 500g)
- Back Bacon (500g)
- Crème Fraiche (500ml)
- Double Cream (500ml)
- Sweetcorn (680g)
- Mushrooms (500g)
- Brie Cheese (400g)

The Way

- Tbsp olive oil in the frying pan, and chop the bacon into small pieces
- Add the bacon and cook until nicely pinked. If everyone is happy with mushrooms you can cook them with the bacon. If not, get them going in a separate pan, either using olive oil or butter as you prefer
- Once the bacon is cooked, drain off any excess oil. Stir in the Double Cream and the Crème Fraiche - you can use either on their own, but we prefer a mixture of both; sauce is thicker
- Add the sweetcorn and then when the mixture is good and hot, add the Brie Cheese, again cut up into bite size pieces
- The cheese pieces not only add flavour to the sauce but also become deliciously gooey and most pleasurable to eat
- Boil the linguine pasta alongside for approx 8 – 10 mins. Allow 50g per person
- Serve immediately with some hot, crusty, garlic bread on the side.

***

Salzburger Sauerkraut & Sausages **1 hour tops** **Serves 4**

The Backstory

A lovely warming dish that will be familiar to those who have visited the German and Austrian Alps, very satisfying after a hard day on the slopes and does not have to be served immediately once cooked and can cope with being kept warm for any stragglers enjoying the après ski!

The Gear

- One cooking apple
- One large carrot
- 50g Butter
- Two tbsp white wine
- Four thick slices smoked bacon
- Four frankfurter or knackwurst saus.
- One tsp caraway seeds optional
- One tsp brown sugar
- ½ kilo jar Sauerkraut (A cheat I know but who wants to shred cabbage after a day's skiing)

The Way

- Preheat oven to 190ºC
- Peel core and grate apple and carrot
- Melt butter in a large oven proof casserole dish and add apple carrot sugar and sauerkraut
- Season with salt and pepper (and caraway) and mix up ingredients well
- Lay bacon on top cover and cook for 40 minutes
- Remove lid and arrange sausages on top and cover and cook for a further 15-20mins.

***

Sledger's Schnitzel **10 mins tops** **Serves 4**

The Backstory

Schnitzel, escalopes or cotelleta these are delicious and very easy to make. Popular with the Kids too! Serve with green salad and new potatoes or with buttered ribbon noodles and seasoned tomato passata.

The Gear

- 150g butter
- Two eggs
- 100g Plain seasoned flour
- 200g Breadcrumbs
- Four 100g Pork or veal fillet
  cut into 1cm deep slices.

The Way

- Cover meat loosely in cling film and gently beat until approx 0.5 cm thick
- Lightly dust each meat portion with the seasoned flour
- Beat the eggs and pour onto a plate
- Put the breadcrumbs on a separate plate
- Coat the meat in egg
- Now coat the meat in breadcrumbs pressing slightly to ensure an even coverage.
- Heat the butter in a large frying pan until foaming
- Fry until golden brown on each side (approx 1-11/2 mins per side)

***

Peter's Pasta   **35 mins tops**   **Serves 6**

The Backstory

Peter X is a friend of ours who works for HM Customs, so we have a real "duty" (Sic) to include one of his recipes in the book. Seriously though, even though he works in a profession that is not universally popular, he's a lovely guy with a sunny outlook on life. This recipe was born when Peter was posted to Belfast some years back and he thought it up while running up the side of Belfast Loch. Working away from home, he was keeping himself fit – in his own words, "This one's tasty and full of Carbs". An ideal description of a meal for hungry skiers. We got this recipe from him after a rather splendid evening in the Builders Arms...

The Gear

- 500g Fusilli or Farfale – multi-coloured tricolore twists
- 4 large Chicken Breasts
- 2 pack of lean back bacon
- 4 ripe sliced avocados
- Juice from 2 full limes
- 2 large red onions
- Salt and Pepper to taste
- Olive oil of course!

The Way

- Grill the bacon until fairly crisp – set aside
- Boil the pasta, 8 – 12 mins (check the packet)
- Roughly chop the onions and cut chicken into large (ish) cubes
- Fry both the chicken and onions together in olive oil
- In a large serving dish, put in alternating layers of pasta then chicken & bacon
- Add the sliced avocado on top and grill for a few minutes to soften
- Serve with a really dry chilled white wine and garlic Ciabatta bread

***

Andermatt Alpler Macaroni   *35 mins tops*   **Serves 6**

The Backstory

This is a very common dish in the Swiss Alps and although it has similarities to a traditional macaroni cheese it is not the same, it is much lighter and is usually served accompanied by a bowl of apple sauce. This may sound strange but try it; the apple sauce really brings out the flavour of the cheese.

The Gear

- I lb macaroni
- 2 tbsp butter
- One medium white onion finely sliced
- 8fl oz double cream

- 200g Sbrinz or Apenzeller or Gruyère grated
- Pinch Black pepper and salt
- Pinch Nutmeg

The Way

- Preheat oven to 200°C (gas mark 4)
- Cook the macaroni according to packet instructions
- Sauté the onions in the butter until brown
- Warm the cream in a saucepan until simmering.
- Place half the macaroni in an oven proof dish and sprinkle half the grated Gruyère over it
- Repeat with a second layer using the remaining macaroni and cheese
- Pour the hot cream evenly over the macaroni and cheese
- Top with the sautéed onions
- Bake in the oven for 20 mins

Variations - some cantons add ham, bacon and/or potatoes to the dish if you wish to do this add approx 25g of cooked chopped ham or bacon and/or 25g of diced par boiled potato.

For the apple sauce

- 1 ½ lb sour apples
- 1oz butter
- 2 fluid oz apple juice or white wine
- sugar

Peel and slice apples, removing the cores.

Heat the butter in a frying pan and sauté the apples briefly

Sprinkle sugar over them to lightly caramelise them

Add juice or wine - allow to cook gently until all the liquid is absorbed

***

Mountain Lamb   A long time; worth every minute   Serves 4

The Backstory

Delicious, fall off the bone lamb, takes longer than most recipes here but the reward is a hearty, warming meal for all, best enjoyed with a robust Cabernet Sauvignon. There is more than a passing similarity to the Greek/Cypriot version of Kleftiko and this as close as we could get to our old friends Loukas and Ramos' creation.

The Gear

- 4 lamb shanks
- One bottle red wine
- One large white onion roughly chopped
- Two stalks celery roughly chopped
- Two carrots roughly chopped
- One leek roughly chopped
- Two Bay leaves
- Two cloves garlic crushed
- Small sprig rosemary (or if dried half teaspoon)

The Way

- Put all ingredients in a large oven/hob proof pot and leave to marinade for 24 hours
- Pre heat oven to 150°C
- After marinating bring to the boil on the stove top
- Once boiling transfer to the oven and cook for 4 - 4½ hours
- Set meat aside and keep warm
- Pour remaining ingredients through a sieve and reduce sauce by half by boiling in a saucepan
- Once sauce reduced pour over lamb and serve with potatoes and vegetables.

Mountain Lamb – worth every minute!

***

Ashley's Pesto Pasta　　　　**Time　8 mins**　　　　**Serves 8**

The Backstory

Basically this meal is the quickest, easiest, healthiest "fast-food" in the kitchen. In the time it takes to cook the pasta, the salad should be ready to go. It's great to watch Ashley cook, he is happy as Larry in the kitchen and throws the ingredients in with a cheerful disposition – perhaps if he wasn't an expert airline avionics engineer, he would have been just as successful as a chef in a top London restaurant. But probably without all the histrionics...

The Gear

- 100g pasta per person (that's 800g of pasta – large pan needed)

- Jar of green Pesto sauce
- Large cucumber chopped
- Some small cherry tomatoes
- Hard boiled eggs
- Plenty of leaves, rocket or lettuce
- Chopped celery
- Some chopped red, yellow, green peppers

The Way

- Pasta on to boil – 8 minutes normally, but check the package instructions
- Chop and mix the salad together
- Drain the cooked pasta and whiz in the jar of pesto – stir with gusto
- Serve with a flourish!
- Could not be easier...

***

4 BLUE PISTE - MAINS

T-Bar Tarragon Chicken   **about 50 mins**   **Serves 6**

The Backstory

This is one of Sister-in-Law Natalie's recipes - her daughter Elena says *"Mummy skis like a Princess!"* It must hold the record for the most requested recipe of all time, whoever eats this at Nat's table says immediately, "Ooh Natalie, you MUST give me the recipe for this, it's incredible!" We know you will think so too ☺. It works best if you leave the chicken to soak overnight in the marinade mixture in the fridge – see below. Little kids like it best without the chilli powder. Can be served with salad and/or potatoes, or rice or pasta.

The Gear

- 6 Chicken Breast fillets
- 8 tbsp lemon juice
- 2 rounded tbsp Paprika
- 1 clove Garlic
- Lots of fresh Tarragon (dried Tarragon works too but flavour weaker)
- 2 oz unsalted butter
- 10 sundried tomatoes
- 300ml double cream (or Crème Fraiche if you have to or can't get Double Cream)
- ½ tsp chilli powder – don't overdo it, this dish has oodles of flavour anyway

T-Bar Tarragon Chicken – reducing the sauce

T-Bar Tarragon Chicken – ready for the table

The Way

- Slice the chicken into strips, place in a bowl with the lemon juice, Paprika, chopped Tarragon and crushed garlic. Cover and leave for at least 30 mins or even overnight!
- Melt the butter in a large deep heavy based pan over a fairly low heat, add chicken and cook gently for 10 mins occasional stir. Slice the tomatoes while this is going on
- Take out the chicken and bubble the juices till reduced – take off the heat & stir in the double cream, bring back to the boil stirring for 2-3mins. Season & add chilli powder
- Return chicken to pan and add sundried tomatoes, heat up for 2mins and serve.
- Better still, cook it the day before, fridge overnight and reheat next day or you can cook it then leave it covered in the oven on low heat for up to an hour.

***

Boarders Baked Chicken w/Cheese   55 mins max   Serves 4

The Backstory

A warming, filling, tasty dish, just the sort of thing to give the hungry snowboarders at the end of a physical, fun packed day. Serving with carrots and green beans is best.

The Gear

- 4 chicken breast fillets - cut into 1 inch chunks
- 2 tbsp vegetable oil
- 25g mushrooms - sliced somewhat thinly
- 100g Gruyere cheese – gr8td ;-)
- 450ml full fat milk
- Half dozen eggs – beaten up
- 200g thick sliced white bread, chopped into 1 inch cubes

- 20g chopped parsley

The Way

- Lightly grease a 1.5 litre baking dish, and then use a fork to beat up the eggs and milk in a large bowl. In go the bread cubes, ¾ of the cheese, parsley and ground black pepper
- Preheat the oven to 190C. Then heat half the oil in a big frying pan, brown-off the chicken (5 mins), then dry off on kitchen roll. Fry the somewhat thinly sliced mushrooms (4 mins) until softening and also dry on kitchen roll
- Stir mushrooms and chicken into the eggy, bread mixture and then pour the whole lot into the baking dish. Scatter the rest of the cheese on top and bake for 30-35 mins until golden brown and risen
- Leave to stand for 5 mins before serving

***

La Plagne Lasagne   55 mins ish   Serves 8

The Backstory

After a hard day's skiing, you can't beat a beautiful, meaty Lasagne which gives off such wonderful aromas from the kitchen while they are all having showers and baths. The smell of baking basil combined with melting cheese and garlic, wafting from the kitchen, produces a most positive reaction from hungry skiers we have found. It is best to serve this with a nice "cross rocket" salad. See the green piste section – where else would we put the salads? Oh and we DO love La Plagne BTW. And of course we love Lasagne too...

The Gear

- A box (about 10 or 12) dried pasta sheets
- 1 large finely chopped onion
- One handful of mushrooms finely chopped
- 2 large jars of Tomato Dolmio or Ragu sauce
- 2 tsp Olive's Oil

- 1 kilo fresh minced beef
- A big handful of fresh basil, chopped quite coarse (or 2 tsp dried basil)
- 400g grated cheese
- 200g of lardons (chopped bacon)
- 4 cloves garlic – crush 'em baby!
- Fresh black pepper and salt to season

White Sauce

- 60g butter
- 60g plain flour
- 500ml milk

The Way

- In a large pan with the olive oil, cook the onions until they start to soften, stirring all the while. Now add the mushrooms so they release their juices and there is coalescence with the crushed garlic. Preheat the oven to 180 degrees Celsius
- Brown the mince and bacon lardons in a frying pan then add to the onions and mushroom mixture – stir in the jars of Dolmio/Ragu sauce – simmer
- Add the chopped basil and season with salt & pepper, stirring the while
- Make the white sauce – very slowly melt the butter in a small pan over a low heat, once done add and mix in the flour a little at a time, stirring all the time, until a light brown paste called a 'roux' is formed, (nothing to do with Australian animals, note the spelling) now very carefully stir in the milk while OFF the heat until a really smooth creamy mixture results, slightly thickened, to which you can stir in half of the cheese – leave half to scatter on the top
- A large, deep, greased ovenproof dish now appears before you as if put there by the assistant chef and you can now *lovingly* layer the lasagne into it – feel the lurve!!
- Start with a layer of the meat mixture, then a layer of pasta sheets, break them to fit the corners if you need to, then a layer of cheese sauce, then layer of meat, then pasta sheets. Basically you'll get about three layers and you're done. Cheese on top, then in the oven for 30 mins, until Golden Brown ☺

La Plagne Lasagne – with a glass for the chef

***

Duckfoot Stroganoff   **1hr 45mins**   **Serves 8**

The Backstory

Now old man Louis, (the Orthodontist) used to make a mean Beef Stroganoff, but as kids we were always revolted by the ingredient *'Sour Cream'*, "Yikes! DAD! You cannot be SERIOUS!?" we cried, but how naïve were we? This recipe became one of our favourites. Braised meats with sour cream are typical of Russian medieval cookery and some of the Stroganoff recipes date back to the 1860s. This one is great served on a bed of rice or with noodles if you prefer.

The Gear

- 1.5 kilos lean stewing beef – cut into strips or cubes, you choose
- 6 rashers of bacon – chopped small
- 2 cloves garlic – mashed

- 450 mls sour cream – Yikes!
- 1 tsp dried marjoram
- 1 large onion – finely chopped
- 150 mls dry white wine – have a glass yourself, why don't you?
- 3 tsps freshly chopped parsley
- paprika
- 2 tsps salt
- ½ tsp pepper – ahh...Aaaaaahhhh...CHOO!!!

The Way

- Brown the diced bacon in a deep heavy based pan, then remove it and put to one side
- The pan should contain bacon residue – lovely. To this you should add the beef and brown the meat on all sides, then sling in the onion and garlic, cooking for about 5 mins until the onion is just tender
- Add the bacon, marjoram, salt and pepper and of course the wine. Stirring the while, bring to the boil then cover and simmer for 1½ hours when the beef should be tender
- Check periodically, give an occasional stir and add a little water if required
- When ready, add the sour cream stirring it in and heat through
- Fresh parsley and paprika sprinkled on top completes the dish

✳✳✳

Stiffy Air Baked Fennel-Salmon   1hr or thereabouts   Serves 8

The Backstory

Fennel and Salmon are such a great combination, but it is not a herb that is commonly eaten. When we have made this one in the past, you can guarantee that someone will say, "Wow! WHAT are those wonderful seeds? They really complement the fish..." Oh indeed they do!

The Gear

- 8 salmon fillets – ideally lightly smoked, skinless & boneless
- 300 mls single cream
- 50g melted butter
- 1.5 kilos potatoes, skins on, washed and sliced nice and thin
- 200 mls dry white wine – Oh go on, have another glass while you're cooking

- 30g freshly chopped dill (leave the dill out if people don't like it)
- 2 tsp Fennel seeds
- Salt & pepper to season

Base layer of potatoes

Oven ready

Fennel-Salmon done

The Way

- The oven is preheated to 190 degrees Celsius
- Boil the potatoes for 4 mins until just tender, drain and rinse under the cold tap, then slice thinly leaving skins on
- Take an ovenproof dish and smear with some of the melted butter
- Now add the base layer of potatoes, sprinkle over w/butter, scatter w/fennel seeds
- Season on top of this with salt & pepper, then place the fish evenly on top
- The cream, wine and dill mixed together come next, pouring this over the fillets
- Add the rest of the potatoes evenly on top, more butter brushed over them, then scatter remaining fennel seeds and add more seasoning if required
- In the oven now for 45 or 50 mins or until the top is crinkly & salmon cooked through
- Best served with another green vegetable such as peas, broccoli, beans or maybe some salad

***

Roasted Vegetables & Couscous   1hr 30mins   Serves 8

The Backstory

We first had Couscous while motorcycling in the South of France back in 1982 and at the time it seemed very exotic – well we were young then and *everything* was exotic. This staple food from the region of North Africa had crept onto the menus of French restaurants in the south at this time – now of course it is everywhere. We like ours with roasted vegetables.

The Gear

- 800g carrots, 800g parsnips, 1 kilo small potatoes, 4 small red onions – the stars of the show!
- 10 tbsps Olive's Oil
- A little white wine vinegar
- 1 kilo of couscous
- 200g raisins

- 200g chopped watercress
- 2 tins of chickpeas
- 250g fresh rocket leaves, chopped
- 150g toasted pine nuts
- 250mls lemon juice
- Big handful of fresh coriander, fresh mint and fresh flat leaf parsley
- Some (20g) fresh thyme leaves
- 2 tbsp Harissa paste
- Large pinch of saffron

The Way

- Preheat the oven to 180 degrees Celsius
- Trim the carrots and halve/trim the parsnips, wash & cut tatties into same size pieces
- Peel & split onions into wedgelike shapes, open out but, leave attached at the base
- Now put all the veg onto a large piece of foil covering a large roasting tray
- Oil and vinegar – drizzle over the top of them all
- Add a handful of fresh chopped parsley and a few thyme leaves
- Now sprinkle with plenty of seasoning and then toss it all over
- Bring the foil up to form a little house over the top
- Roast for 30 mins, then uncover and roast for a further 30, tossing occasionally
- While all this is going on, cook the couscous as per the instructions on the packet, normally twice the volume of water to couscous, with the harissa, saffron and raisins
- When it's done, add the roasted veggies, chickpeas, pine nuts, chopped rocket, watercress, lemon juice and herbs, and then mix it all together. A splash of olive oil to the mix will help prevent the grains from sticking together
- Keep it all warm in the oven till ready to serve – works well reheated the next day too! (and even the day after that...)

***

The "No-Worry" Curry (Lamb)　　1 hr 30 (ish)　　Serves 8

The Backstory

We've tried plenty of curries over the years, but this is one of the easiest and reliable recipes. Don't forget to chill a few lager beers for the chaps and wine for the ladies. – some people prefer Naan or other breads to Rice. Our thanks to the chef at the Leela Kempinsky in Mumbai.

Grinding Cardamom pods

Mix the two together then it's Oven ready – no-worries!

The Gear

- 1½ kilos lean lamb off the bone
- 10 tbsps Olive's Oil
- 4 tsp granulated sugar
- 2 large onions finely chopped
- 2 tsps grated nutmeg
- 2 tsps chilli powder
- 2 tsps ground cardamom
- 2 tbsp dry mustard powder
- 4 cloves garlic – crush 'em baby!
- 2 tbsp ground coriander
- 4 tsp salt
- 2 large tins of tomatoes (2 x 400g)

The Way

- Preheat the oven to 180 degrees Celsius
- Cut the lamb up into 1 inch (2.4 cm) pieces and place in a large ovenproof dish
- Now put the rest of the gear in a large bowl and mix well – pour over the meat
- Give it all a stir, then cover the dish and whack it into the oven for about 75 mins
- Stir once or twice during the cooking, then skim off excess fat prior to serving
- Serve with boiled rice, pilau rice or Naan and the usual curry bits and pieces

"No-Worry" Curry, job done

Pip's Posh Poultry **Approx 50 Mins** **Serves 4-6**

The Backstory

Thanks to Great Aunty Pip for this one. No she's not called that because she's "old", it's just because she's ***"Great!"*** Seriously though, she has the wickedest sense of humour and is always fun to be with - add to that, she's a brilliant cook.

The Gear

- 4 Chicken Breasts, skinned & deboned
- ¼ tsp. (1 ml) Pepper
- 3 tbsps.(45 ml) Oil
- 1 – 10 oz (280 g) Fresh Asparagus or Broccoli (can use frozen)
- 1 – 10 oz (284 ml) Can Cream of Chicken Soup
- ½ cup (125 ml) Mayonnaise
- 1 tsp. (5 ml) Curry Powder
- 1 tsp. (5 ml) Lemon Juice
- 1 cup (250 ml)   Grated Cheddar Cheese

The Way

- Cut chicken into 2 inch x 4 inch pieces and sprinkle with pepper.
- Sauté slowly in oil, medium heat until white / opaque. After 6 minutes - drain.
- Cook asparagus/broccoli until tender/crisp, drain and arrange in bottom of buttered 7" (18 cm) diameter casserole.
- Place chicken on top.
- Mix soup, mayonnaise, curry and lemon juice together and pour over chicken.
- Sprinkle top with Cheese and bake uncovered at (190 C) for 30 to 35 minutes.
- Serve with egg noodles or rice and a favourite salad.
- This recipe doubles well for larger groups.

***

Lambdango **Straight One Hour (easy)** **Serves 6**

The Backstory

Cue the music, *"SAY!... Can you do the Lamdango...?"* Another of Pip's treasures this one, straight from the frozen wastes of Canada – you gotta try it. A lovely winter warmer of a recipe that gets all the juices flowing.

The Gear

- 1 lb Ground Lamb
- 1 Medium Onion, Chopped
- 10-15 Small button mushrooms, washed and cut in half
- 1 or 2 Garlic cloves, crushed
- 1 Tsp. Oregano
- 1 or 2 – 10 oz. packages frozen Chopped Spinach, thawed and drained well
- 1- 10 oz. can Cream of Celery Soup
- 1- Cup (150ml) Sour Cream - Crème Fraiche works just as well.
- 1- Tbsp. Uncooked Minute Rice Salt and Pepper to taste
- 6 oz. pkg. Grated Mozzarella Cheese

The Way

- Brown meat, onions, mushrooms, garlic and oregano in a frying pan.
- Stir in spinach, soup, sour cream, rice, salt and pepper to taste.
- Put mixture in casserole dish. Place cheese on top.
- Bake in 350 degree oven for 35 to 45 minutes.
- If you are a cheese fan, double the amount called for and layer this in the middle of the casserole.

***

Ionian Moussaka   1 hr 30 mins approx   Serves 8

The Backstory

We are always on the lookout for recipes while abroad and this one we found in a lovely little restaurant while sailing from Corfu in the Ionian Sea a few years back. The natural harbour of Lakka in the northern part of the island of Paxos is a stunning location and as we dropped Lady Lavinia's anchor in the middle of the bay, we knew we would be having a great meal here – we were right! We had ours with green salad and garlic bread. Put Lakka, Paxos island on your bucket list – it's an awesome spot.

The Gear

- 1 kilo lean minced lamb
- 1 kilo aubergines, thinly sliced
- 2 x 400g tins plum tomatoes – chopped
- 2 onions – chop 'em fine me hearties
- ½ tsp ground cinnamon
- 2 cloves garlic – peeled and finalé chopped
- 2 tbsp tomato purée
- 450g Greek yoghurt
- 2 eggs
- 50g gr8td parmesan
- Small handful fresh chopped parsley
- Salt and pepper to season

The Way

- Using a large frying pan, brown off the meat with the onion and garlic for 5 mins
- Then stir in the, tinned tommies, cinnamon, puree and seasoning
- Bring it all to the boil, add the parsley and then simmer for 15 mins (ish)
- Layer half the sliced aubergines on the base of a large ovenproof dish and then add half the meat mixture – repeat this stage with the next layer, aubergines then meat
- Using a small bowl, mix the eggs, yoghurt, seasoning and half the parmesan cheese
- Pour this mixture on top and sprinkle with the remainder of the cheese
- Into the oven now for 40 mins – the top should be nice and brown

Gaper Goulash   **1¼ hrs approx**   **Serves 8**

The Backstory

A 'Gaper' is a skier who stops, rests and takes in the scenery. With us more, erm... "mature" skiers, that's not such a bad thing is it? After all... it gives the youngsters time to catch us up!! LOL!!

The Gear

- ½ kilo of lean stewing beef – cut into 3cm cubes
- 2 onions, chopped
- 1 parsnip peeled n chopped
- 1 large potato – cubed
- 1 carrot, peeled n chopped
- 1 celery stalk – chopped
- 1 x 400g tin tomatoes
- 1 green pepper – deseeded n diced
- 2 tbsp Olive's Oil
- 3 tbsp paprika
- ½ litre beef stock
- 6 tbsp sour cream
- Fresh parsley to garnish
- 3 cloves garlic – crushed
- 2 tsp caraway seeds

The Way

- In a large pan, heat the oil and brown off the beef – 5 mins should be enough
- Now add the chopped onion and caraway seeds and sauté away – until soft
- Pop in the paprika, stir a for a minute, then add the beef stock
- Bring pan to boil, stirring continuously, then simmer for 40 mins stirring occasionally
- After about 35 or 40 mins, meat should be tender, add tommies, veggies and garlic
- 25 mins more simmering should be enough to tenderise those veggies
- Keep stirring occasionally during this last bit and then serve hot, top off with dollops of sour cream and garnish with parsley – you've made the coolest goulash in the valley, yum, yum!

Side-cut Chicken with Brie   35 mins tops   Serves 8

The Backstory

This is a recipe which will endow the ski chalet chef with a reputation approaching Cordon Bleu standards and yet it is really so easy to make. It relies heavily upon those old chestnuts, chicken, mushrooms and oregano which always work so well together in a dish. As indicated below, this one is delicious when served with Asparagus and baby new potatoes.

The Gear

- 8 chicken breast fillets
- 600g mushrooms
- A large Brie cheese
- Olive's Oil
- 2 tsps oregano
- Large bunch of asparagus – enough for 6 spears each
- 2 kilos of baby new potatoes

The Way

- Preheat the oven to 180 degrees Celsius
- Wash and slice the mushrooms, then sauté them for a few mins in a frying pan
- Prepare the chicken breasts with a sharp knife making a slit (side-cut) in each one
- Insert a slice of brie into each of the side-cut breasts –brie should be cut ½ cm thick
- Smear Olive Oil on the base of an ovenproof dish and lay the chicken breasts on it
- Sprinkle then with oregano and spoon the mushrooms all over the top
- Bake for 25 or 30 mins in the middle of the oven
- While this is going on, trim the bottoms off the asparagus spears, then steam for 10 mins over boiling water. While the steaming is happening, scrub the tatties and boil in their skins – simmer gently for 20 mins, they should be just like your first ever ski instructor, firm but tender! ☺

Chicken Mishmash   **35 mins tops**   **Serves 8**

The Backstory

This recipe came originally from our good friend Jessica Gardner (Ashley's Mum). It is a real favourite with the kids – yes and big kids too, all the adults like it! It's not often that you crack that special challenge trying to find a meal which appeals to all ages – but this does it every time!

Chicken Mishmash

Jessica Gardner

The Gear

- 8 boneless chicken breasts, cubed (1 inch cubes) and cooked
- 2 cups grated cheese
- 2 cups mayonnaise
- 2 cans concentrated cream of chicken soup
- 1 green pepper – deseeded and finely chopped
- 1 red pepper – deseeded and chop, chop, chop
- 2 onions – peeled and chopped
- 2 sticks of celery – trimmed and chopped

- 2 bags crisps
- 2 tbsps Olive's Oil
- Salt & fresh ground black pepper

The Way

- Preheat the oven to 180 degrees Celsius
- Gently fry the onions & peppers in a little olive oil to soften them up
- In a large bowl, mix all together (leaving out the cheese and crisps) adding salt & pepper
- Put all in a greased dish, then on the top add the crushed crisps with the grated cheese
- Bake at 180 degrees until the top is lightly brown about 25 mins

Grandma's Gnocchi　　　　　　**35 mins**　　　　　**Serves 4**

The Backstory

Gnocchi was always a family favourite in Berni's dad's house when he was growing up and he passed on the cheese sauce recipe, Gnocchi is so versatile and can go with many other sauces as an alternative to cheese and is also very filling.

The Gear

- 800g Gnocchi
- 100g Broccoli cut into small florets
- 100g Cauliflower cut into small florets
- 100g Cherry tomatoes halved
- 25g Pecorino/parmesan cheese grated
  For the cheese sauce

- 25g unsalted butter
- half white onion, finely chopped
- One garlic clove, finely chopped
- 50ml white wine
- 200ml double cream
- 100g Pont l'Evêque/brie or Camembert cheese, chopped

- salt and freshly ground black pepper

The Way

- Cook Gnocchi according to packet instructions
- Pre heat grill to high
- Cook broccoli and cauliflower in salted boiling water for 5 minutes
- Heat the butter in a frying pan over a medium heat and fry the onion and garlic until soft.
- Add the white wine and simmer until reduced by half
- Add the double cream and simmer gently
- Stir in the cheese, season well with salt and freshly ground black pepper and warm until cheese is completely melted. Season with salt and plenty of black
- Drain gnocchi and vegetables and place in shallow oven proof dish
- Scatter with cherry tomatoes and cover with cheese sauce mix in gently with a spoon so everything is covered in sauce
- Now scatter Pecorino/Parmesan over the top and grill on high until golden

    Variations: - You can use tortellini instead of gnocchi if preferred. Also the addition of chopped smoked bacon pieces is very nice just add 2-4 rashers of chopped cooked smoked bacon at stage 7 after cheese has melted.

***

Wilhelm's cheese fondue **20 mins** **Serves 4-6**

The Backstory

Berni's father used to always make a cheese fondue on Christmas Eve as an alternative to the buffet meal which they ate in the Swiss tradition after opening their presents. It is still a family favourite not just on Christmas Eve but throughout the winter months. Beware though; tradition says that if you drop a piece of bread off your fork into the mixture and it is lost by a man, he must buy a bottle of wine - if such a thing happens to a woman, she must kiss the man on her left... It is also highly recommended to drink plenty of white wine with this dish, we would recommend a dry Reisling, for the teetotal a cup of green tea also makes a great accompaniment (Hot drinks or alcohol are said to help break down the cheese and aid digestion).

Wilhelm's Cheese Fondue

The Gear

- 250g Gruyere grated
- 250g Emmental grated
- 25g brie rind removed chopped(optional)
- One clove garlic pressed
- One garlic clove halved
- Three tablespoons kirsch

- 250 ml dry white wine
- Pinch ground nutmeg
- Pinch black pepper
- Two teaspoons cornflower

The Way

- Rub the halved garlic clove around the fondue pot (make sure pot is ceramic as a metal one will burn the cheese)
- Add the wine and lemon juice and heat gently until simmering
- Add the Gruyere and Emmental
- Slowly heat the cheese mixture stirring frequently (do not boil) until all melted
- Mix the kirsch and the cornflower together
- Add the kirsch mixture to the cheese mixture and cook for a further 2minutes stirring frequently
- Now add brie and stir until completely melted in (this is optional but gives a lovely creamy taste to the fondue)
- Season with salt, pepper and nutmeg

  Serve with cubes of crusty bread and sliced gherkins

***

Slalom Salmon   **20 mins**   **Serves 4-6**

The Backstory

Most large towns will have a fish section in the supermarkets, so if you can find a nice piece of Salmon the following will make a welcome change from cheese or red meats.

The Gear

- One medium leek
- Two cloves garlic
- 200g crème fraiche
- 50g frozen peas

- Chopped parsley
- Spaghetti or taleteller
- 100g Smoked salmon ribbons/trimmings
- One tablespoon Olive oil
- Handful pine nuts (optional)

The Way

- Cook pasta according to packet instructions
- Slice the leek thinly and fry slowly in the olive oil until soft
- Add the frozen peas to the pasta approximately 5-10 minutes before pasta ready and cook until both ready
- Crush garlic and add to leeks continue to cook on low heat for a further 2 minutes
- Add the smoked salmon and stir continue to cook for 1-2 minutes
- Drain pasta and peas
- Add the crème fraiche to the salmon and leek mixture and stir
- Add the drained peas and pasta to the mixture mix and serve topped with a few pine nuts and a sprig of parsley

***

Monte Bre meatballs in tomato sauce   1 hour   Serves 6

The Backstory

A real hit for the whole family! This is a very tasty variation on a theme especially when teamed up with your favourite pasta. Seriously the kids cannot get enough of this, it is regular favourite at home even when we are nowhere near a mountain.

The Gear

- 900g mince (beef, lamb or pork)
- Two finely chopped white onions
- 60g breadcrumbs
- 2 eggs
- 1.2kg chopped tomatoes
- 4 tablespoons Honey
- 4 tablespoons Sugar
- 4 tablespoons Malt Vinegar

- 4 tablespoons Worcester sauce (soy sauce or maggi is a suitable alternative if not available
- Salt and freshly ground pepper
- Soured cream (optional)

The Way

- Preheat oven to 220°C
- Mix mince with onion breadcrumbs and eggs season with salt and pepper
- Form approx 24 balls with your hands
- Mix tomatoes with eight tablespoons of water, Worcester sauce, honey, sugar and vinegar
- Drizzle olive oil into an ovenproof dish place in meatballs and cover with sauce
- Don't worry about drowning the meatballs most of the sauce gets absorbed
- Cook in the oven for 30-40 minutes serve with boiled rice or buttered spaghetti and a smidge of soured cream

Monte Bre Meatballs

Berni Chetham

5 RED PISTE - MAINS

Traditional Tartiflette   **70 mins (& worth it)**   **Serves 6**

The Backstory

Here we go, one of the most traditional dishes of the French Alps. A little bit high in calorie content of course, but remember where you are - the mountains. This is the place where the locals have to live and work at high altitude all through the winter and it takes no time at all to burn off calories, <u>especially if you are out all day doing winter sports!</u> Go for it.

The Gear

- 8 rashers (250g ish) of smoked bacon, rindless, chopped
- 1kg large potatoes, skins left on, thinly sliced
- 1 large onion – sliced (oh so thinly)
- 300ml fresh semi-skimmed milk
- 250ml double cream – if not available, crème Fraiche will do
- 1 garlic clove – crush me baby!
- 8g fresh thyme – dried will do if you have to
- 250g Reblochon cheese, sliced thinly – a speciality of Savoie & Haute Savoie
- A little vegetable oil

The Way

- Fry the bacon & onion over a medium heat in the oil for 4 or 5 mins
- Chop the fresh thyme and add with the cream, milk and garlic to a large pan, simmer
- Now add the potatoes, mix up a little and simmer for 5 mins, Preheat oven to 180C
- Now stir in the onions and bacon mixture & season with fresh ground black pepper

- Lightly grease a 1.5 litre ovenproof dish, then place half the potato mixture in the bottom, then add a layer of half the sliced cheese, then the next layer of potato mixture, finishing off with a layer of cheese on the top
- In the oven now for 40 to 45 mins – the top should be a golden brown colour
- Garnish with a few sprigs of fresh thyme if you remembered to keep any back
- Best served with salad and some chunks of French bread – gorgeous!

***

Don't forget to be artistic with the cheeseboard

***

French Boeuf **15 mins prep/2½ hrs cooking** **Serves 8**

The Backstory

The French may call us "Les Ros Bif!", but when it comes to putting beef on the table, they don't do so badly themselves. In many areas of France, beef is their most popular red meat for dinner. This recipe sourced from French friends typifies the way they do it. Bon Appetit! This dish is delicious served with steamed veggies, such as cauliflower, broccoli and rice.

The Gear

- 2 kilos lean stewing beef
- 3 medium onions – chopped quite fine
- 3 tbsp red wine vinegar
- 200mls hot beef stock – one beef stock cube in boiling water
- 3 tbsp plain flour
- 1½ tsp light muscovado sugar
- 1½ pints of Guinness
- 3 tbsp French wholegrain mustard
- 1 French stick – sliced diagonally
- 1 sachet of bouquet garni
- 3 tbsp Olive's Oil
- 3 cloves of garlic – use whole

The Way

- Preheat the oven to 150 degrees Celsius
- Using the oil, in a large pan, brown off the meat for 3 or 4 mins then set aside
- Now fry the onions in some oil for a few mins, stirring the while, and then add the flour, sugar and vinegar. Add half the Guinness, stir it all up and then transfer to a metal casserole dish, adding the beef stock and the rest of the Guinness
- Bring to the boil stirring all the time then reduce the heat and simmer for 5 mins
- Add the beef and stir in some seasoning, put in the bouquet garni and garlic
- Now cover the casserole dish and put it in the oven for 2 hours – beef must be tender

- Remove casserole from the oven, discard the bouquet and garlic, turn oven up to 220
- Cover each slice of French bread with the mustard and put the slices on top of the casserole, sticky side up
- Back in the oven now for 15 mins at 220 degrees Celsius – Voila! Le Boeuf; French style.

Reminded us of the Cow in

"The Restaurant at the end of the Universe"

(By Douglas Adams)

***

Lady Lavinia Stifado   **20 mins prep/5 hrs cook**   **Serves 6**

The Backstory

The yacht which we sailed for several summers in Greece, gives its name to this dish and is inspired by the delicious meal we had in Bob's father-in-law's tiny restaurant, just outside Gouvia marina in Corfu. Bob married Litsa a local girl and together they run their own sailing fleet of rental yachts – check out their website www.bobsyachts.gr   An ideal slow cook recipe, you can put it in the oven at lunchtime, ski all afternoon, waltz in 5 hours later and it's done!

S/V Lady Lavinia

The Gear

- 1 kilo lean stewing beef 1 inch cubed (2.4cm)
- 5 cloves chopped garlic
- 1 kilo chopped onions

- 100mls Olive's Oil
- 1 kilo plum tomatoes, peeled n chopped – see below
- 50mls tomato puree
- 250mls red wine

The Way

- Preheat the oven to 150 degrees Celsius – low temperature, slow cooking dish
- Score the tomato skins, put them in a bowl, pour over boiling water from kettle – leave for 1 min then drain, rinse in cool water, then peel with sharp knife
- Using half the olive oil, gently sauté the onions n garlic until tender - about 15 mins
- Now place them in a large, deep ovenproof dish
- With the remaining oil, brown off the meat – 5 or 7 mins
- Pour the meat into the casserole dish and stir in with the tommies and the puree
- Add the wine and season with some salt and ground black pepper
- Put the lid on the casserole and whack it in the oven for 5 hours
- After this time the meat should be tender and the juices all reduced
- Best served with very plain veggies and/or a plain green salad
- "Shiver me timbers me hearties" – Captain Jack Sparrow would love this meal!

***

Marbella Mackerel Risotto   **40 mins**   **Serves 8**

The Backstory

Another of our mate Peter's recipes – he calls this one "Poor man's Paella". He said he wanted to do a Paella, but when he looked in the fridge all they had was some Mackerel – this was the result and it works. You can substitute the Mackerel with Chorizo and Bacon – a great alternative. Warm crusty bread is tops with this one.

The Gear

- 500g of Risotto Rice (Arboretto Proper) – washed
- 2 glasses of dry white wine
- 4 cloves garlic - crushed
- 2 fish or veggie stock cubes to make one litre of stock
- 2 large onions
- 1 tsp Turmeric
- 10 tomatoes cut into large chunks
- 4 packs of peppered or plain Mackerel
- Olive oil again of course

The Way

- In the oil, fry the onions and garlic gently
- Add the rice and stir into the onions and garlic
- 1 or 2 minutes on a high heat then add the Turmeric and stir
- Stir in the 2 glasses of wine – expect a satisfying "SSShhhhhhhhh!!!" from the pan
- Add all of the stock (1 litre) in three stages – stir it in
- Turn down and simmer, don't worry it looks like watery soup
- After 5 – 7 minutes stir in the tomatoes
- Further 10 minutes simmering (stirring regularly) put in chunks of Mackerel
- Layer the Mackerel on top at first, fold fish in carefully, try not to break up
- After a further 5 mins simmering, now taste the rice
- If a little dry, add more wine. Season to taste with Salt and Pepper

***

Avalanche Veal **1 hr 20 mins** **Serves 8**

The Backstory

Now not everybody likes Veal and there is a lot of misinformation out there which can be off-putting for some people. On the continent however it is a very popular dish. Remember that nations such as the French and Dutch who have been occupied in wartime are much less squeamish than the rest of us. They will eat every part of an animal for example. Hungry skiers are in the same category I guess! This dish will need some vegetables with it.

The Gear

- 2 kilos of veal – medallions are best, or slices of veal fillet, cut about 2cms thick
- 1 large onion finely chopped
- 300mls chicken stock
- 4 tbsp plain flour
- 100g butter
- 4tsp lemon juice
- 4tsp dried tarragon
- Salt n pepper to season

The Way

- Preheat the oven to 180 degrees Celsius
- Season veal with salt n pepper, then using butter in a frying pan, brown off the meat
- Place veal into shallow ovenproof dish, then in frying pan sauté the onions till soft
- Stir in the plain flour and cook for a minute, before slowly adding milk & chicken stock
- Bring to the boil stirring the while now add tarragon, lemon juice and salt n pepper
- After the sauce is well mixed, pour over meat in the ovenproof dish, cover with lid/foil
- Whizz it into the oven now for approximately 50 mins or until the meat is tender

***

Rutli Ris Casimir **Time** **30 mins** **Serves 4**

The Backstory

Aunty Esther's recipe is loved by all the family. A light curry dish that has a delicate fruity flavour. Popular in Germany, Austria and Switzerland and a kids favourite, in fact a great way to introduce them to spicier food.

The Gear

- 500g pork fillet, veal or chicken cut into small thin pieces
- Two tablespoons sunflower oil
- Two tablespoons flour
- 2 tablespoons mild curry powder
- One white onion finely chopped
- One clove garlic pressed
- 100ml dry white wine
- 100ml pineapple juice
- One apple grated
- 250ml bouillon
- Six - eight slices pineapple chopped into small pieces
- One - two bananas chopped into small pieces
- Handful of maraschino cherries halved with stones removed
- 100ml double cream
- 25g Sliced almond pieces
- 200g Long grain rice

The Way

- With kitchen roll pat dry the meat pieces
- In a large frying pan heat the oil
- Fry the meat gently until lightly browned
- Sprinkle the flour and curry powder over and stir until mixed in
- Add the onion, garlic, white wine, pineapple juice, grated apple and bouillon
- Cook for 10 minutes then taste and season with salt and pepper extra curry powder if required
- Add remaining fruit and heat through gently
- Add the cream and stir through
- Serve sprinkled with the almond pieces & ideal with boiled rice.

***

6 BLUE PISTE - SIDES

Herby Potatoes   **40 mins**   **Serves 4-6**

The Backstory

A great accompaniment to many of the dishes in this collection. But also can be enjoyed on their own.

The Gear

- 750g Waxy type potatoes (like Desiree) peeled and thinly sliced
- Two red onions peeled and thinly sliced
- Six tablespoons olive oil
- 100g Gruyère
- Two tablespoon chopped basil
- Salt and pepper

The Way

- Place the sliced potatoes in a bowl and cover with cold water stand for 10minutes and then drain
- Heat oil in a frying pan
- Add onions and sauté for 2mins turning frequently
- Add potatoes
- Season with salt and pepper
- Sauté turning frequently for 15-20 minutes until tender and golden (try to avoid potatoes breaking up)
- Sprinkle basil over the top and then add cheese
- Cook for a further 2 minutes do not stir serve once the cheese has melted.

***

Rookies Risotto   **40 mins**   **Serves 4 -6**

The Backstory

Very filling and very versatile, risotto can be great as a meal in its own right by adding extras like cooked chicken/bacon pieces, peas, asparagus, peppers etc. towards the end of the cooking process or can be used as an accompaniment to many meat and fish dishes.

The Gear

- 50g Unsalted butter
- One shallot onion finely chopped
- 350g Carnaroli or Arborio rice
- 150ml dry white wine
- 1.2 litres hot vegetable stock
- One tablespoon chopped fresh parsley
- 25g grated parmesan cheese
- Small pinch saffron (optional but gives a nice golden colour)
- Salt and freshly ground black pepper

The Way

- Heat butter in a heavy based saucepan
- Add the shallot and fry for 2-3 minutes
- Stir in rice and coat in the butter (add saffron if desired to give a golden colour)
- Pour in white wine
- And simmer until liquid is absorbed
- Add one ladle full of stock and simmer until absorbed
- Repeat until all stock is absorbed and rice is plump and tender this takes approximately 30 minutes
- Add teaspoon of butter stir and serve with grated parmesan and parsley sprinkled on top.

***

Mountain potatoes   **25 mins**   **Serves 4-6**

The Backstory

A great accompaniment to many other dishes or can be served with a green salad as a meal in its own right.

The Gear

- 1kg Waxy type potatoes
- (like Desiree) peeled and cubed
- 250g smoked bacon cubed
- 250g Abondance cheese sliced
- Quarter litre white wine
- Freshly milled black pepper

The Gear

- Fry the diced onion in a little butter
- Add the potatoes and bacon
- Fry gently for 15 minutes (Do not stir) until potatoes browned a little
- Add the white wine and place cheese on top of potatoes
- Season with pepper and cook on low heat for a further 10 minutes

***

7 GREEN PISTE - DESSERTS

Mont Blanc, Baked Apples   1 hour   Serves 6

The Backstory

The perfect (healthy) way to finish off your evening meal.

The Gear

- Six eating apples cored
- 80g dried mixed fruit chopped
- 50ml brandy
- 30g brown sugar
- Half teaspoon allspice
- 100g butter

The Way

- Preheat oven to 150°C
- Place the mixed dried fruit and the brandy into a bowl and leave to soak for at least two hours, but ideally overnight

Mum and daughter

Mountain Crag Crumble   55 minutes   Serves 4-6

The Backstory

A great way to use up the leftover fruit near the end of your holiday. Any combination is okay but apple, pear and blackberry is delicious. Serve with cream, custard or ice cream.

The Gear

- 800g fruit (apples, pears, plums, peaches, rhubarb, blackberries etc) I wouldn't recommend using banana though it is possible.
- Juice of one lemon
- 225g sugar (golden or brown tastes best)
- One teaspoon mixed spice
- 100g butter chopped into small pieces
- 225g plain flour
- 75g ground almonds or porridge oats

The Way

- Pre heat oven to 200°C
- Peel core and chop fruit as appropriate
- Toss fruit in the lemon juice
- Lightly butter a shallow oven proof dish (1.8L capacity)
- Add the fruit mixture to dish and set to on side
- Put butter and flour into a bowl and gently rub together through fingertips (try to keep hands cool so as not to melt the butter too much) until the mixture looks like fine breadcrumbs
- Add the sugar and almonds/porridge oats and stir into mixture
- Spoon the crumble mixture over the fruit
- Bake in the oven for about 35-45 minutes until fruit is tender and crumble golden.

***

Snow domes   **50 mins**   **Serves 4-6**

The Backstory

Okay, so this pudding is high in calories but you've earned it. Just think of how many calories you burnt off today and then add up tomorrow's exertions, go on you deserve it.

The Gear

- Two medium lemons
- Two tablespoon cream sherry
- Two tablespoons brandy
- 50g caster sugar
- 284ml Double cream
- 6-8 Ginger biscuits
- 50g dark chocolate

The Way

- Grate the lemon rinds into a bowl and then add the juice
- Add the brandy, sherry and sugar and stir until sugar dissolves
- Pour in the cream and whisk until mixture forms soft peaks
- Divide mixture between 4-6 glasses
- Chill for 1 hour
- Serve with a ginger biscuit and some chocolate shavings sprinkled over the top

A great advert for hot chocolate

Titlis Toffee Pudding   **10 mins**   **Serves 4-6**

The Backstory

Be careful how you pronounce this one... A cheat's version of a classic sticky toffee pudding. Very popular with the kids and delicious with a scoop of vanilla ice cream or whipped cream. This dish does need planning ahead as you will find it difficult to get Jamaican ginger cake and golden syrup abroad so we usually take them with us from the UK.

The Gear

- 250g Jamaican ginger cake or Parkin or as a last resort Madeira cake
- 50g Butter
- 100g Brown sugar
- 100g Golden syrup
- 2 drops vanilla extract
- Double cream

The Way

- Preheat the oven to 180°C
- Slice the cake into 1-2cm deep slices and arrange in a shallow oven proof dish
- Melt the butter, sugar and syrup in a saucepan stirring until all sugar dissolves
- Simmer for 5 minutes stirring all the time
- Remove from the heat and stir in the cream and vanilla
- Pour mixture evenly over the cake
- Bake for 10-15 minutes until warmed through and bubbling slightly
- Cool for 5 minutes and serve

***

8 BLUE PISTE - DESSERTS

Berni's Boozy Pears   **30 mins**   **Serves 4**

The Backstory

These are a deliciously light end to a meal and can be served hot or cold. Great served hot with a little of the poaching liquid and vanilla ice cream. When we were writing the first draft of the book, we did re-run some of our old recipes together – this was one of them. There is a photo of us all sat around the table at the end of a lovely meal looking very satisfied with ourselves – glowing red faces etc. We could have renamed this recipe "Berni's Boozy Mates!"

The Gear

- Four ripe but firm pears
 (Comice are ideal)

- Rind from one orange
- Two tablespoons juice
- 500 ml Burgundy wine
- 150g caster sugar
- One cinnamon stick
  Or ½ tsp ground cinnamon

- Four cloves

The Way

- Peel pears leaving stalk on
- Use a corer to remove the core from the pear
- Slice a small section from the pears bottom to help the pears stand upright
- Place all remaining ingredients into a wide saucepan and heat
- Stir until sugar has dissolved
- Add pears, cover and bring to the boil
- Reduce the heat and poach for 20mins spooning liquid over the pears from time to time.

Baguette and Butter Pudding   **50 mins**   **Serves 4-6**

The Backstory

A simple but delicious pudding which uses up day old leftover baguette. Other bread can be used so long as the slices are no thicker than 2 cm and each slice is cut into smaller triangles. Serves four hungry people or six as a light, fluffy dessert.

The Gear

- 14x1-2cm deep slices of day old baguette (or 5x1-2cm deep slices of day old bread cut into triangles)
- 50g currants, sultanas or mixed fruit
- 570ml(1pint) Milk
- 2 medium eggs
- 25g butter
- 2 tablespoons brown sugar
- Quarter teaspoon cinnamon

The Way

- Preheat oven to 190°C
- Evenly butter all the slices of baguette (bread) and arrange slightly overlapping in an oven proof dish
- Scatter mixed fruit over bread placing some between slices
- In a bowl or jug mix sugar egg and milk and beat with a fork for 1 minute
- Now carefully pour mixture over the dry ingredients
- Make sure that all the bread has been moistened with the mixture (if any is still dry use a spoon to drizzle some mixture over).
- Sprinkle the cinnamon evenly over the top of the dish and cover the dish with foil and leave to rest for half an hour
- Place in the oven and cook for approximately 40 minutes.

Topsy Turvy Pineapple Cake   50 mins   Serves 4-6

The Backstory

Great for recovering from life's little ups and downs and looks very impressive in the middle of the dinner table.

The Gear

- One large tin pineapple rings
- One carton glace cherries
- 125g Self raising flour
- 100g Castor sugar
- 100g Butter or margarine
- Two eggs
- 25g brown sugar
- 25g butter

The Way

- Preheat oven to 190°C
- Rub 25g butter all around a small casserole dish then shake in the brown sugar until it coats the butter all around the inside of the dish
- Drain the pineapple and arrange them around the bottom and side of the dish
- Chop glace cherries in half and insert into any gaps between the pineapple.
- In a separate bowl beat sugar and butter together until creamy
- Beat eggs with a fork and add to mixture a bit at a time
- Then fold in the flour gently until all mixed through
- Pour this mixture into the dish making a little dip in the middle
- Bake for 30-40 minutes

***

Cross Country Crepes   15 minutes   Serves 4-6

The Backstory

Everyone likes crepes and these can be filled with sweet or savoury fillings. Some of our favourites are grated gruyere and small smoky bacon bits or nutella and banana pieces. Whatever you fill them with this recipe is easy to make and depending how skilled you are at spreading the mixture thinly around the frying pan you can make between 8-12 crepes.

The Gear

- 60g Plain flour
- 50g Buckwheat or whole-wheat flour
- 2 tablespoons melted butter
- Two large eggs
- 200ml Milk
- 75ml Water
- Pinch of salt
- Butter to cook crepes with

The Way

- If you have a blender put all ingredients into a bowl and whiz together leave to stand for ten minutes and then proceed to step 6
- If not sieve the flour into a bowl make a well in the centre
- Break the eggs into the well beat them with a fork slowly incorporating the flour
- Add the milk and water together in a separate jug and slowly add to the mixture
- Whisk with a fork until the mixture is smooth and the consistency of thin cream.
- Add a teaspoon of butter to the frying pan once foaming add 2-4 tablespoons of mixture depending on the size of frying pan and quickly whizz this around the pan to thinly coat the base
- Cook for 30 seconds to 1 minute until lightly browned
- Using a spatula flip over to the other side, add desired filling (do not overfill) once warmed through fold crepe in half and then into a quarter
- Serve immediately
- Repeat until all mixture is used up

For crepes suzette make up crepes as above but do not fill just put to one side and keep warm

- 150ml orange juice
- Finely grated rind from one orange
- Finely grated rind and juice from one lemon
- One tablespoon caster sugar
- Two tablespoons Grand Marnier
- 50g butter (preferably unsalted)
- Take a large frying pan and melt the butter in it than add the rest of the ingredients and heat gently add the crepes one at a time coating them in the sauce and folding them in half and then into a quarter.
- Once all the crepes are in the pan and coated in the sauce if you wish to be flamboyant you can heat a tablespoon of liqueur and set light to it spooning it over the crepes.

Ski train in the Alps

Blading Brownies   35 minutes   Serves 4-6

The Backstory

The kids favourite. Great served warm from the oven with vanilla ice cream.

The Gear

- 200g good quality milk chocolate broken up
- 200g butter
- 3 eggs
- 112g plain flour
- 250g sugar
- Half teaspoon vanilla essence
- Half teaspoon salt
- 112g chopped nuts (optional)

The Way

- Line a 8x 12" baking tray with baking paper
- Melt butter and chocolate gently in a pan or in the microwave taking care not to burn the chocolate
- Beat sugar and eggs in a separate bowl ideally with a blender for 2 minutes
- Now add the chocolate mixture to the egg mixture and stir in using a spoon
- Sift in the flour salt and vanilla and stir
- Add the chopped nuts if required
- Pour into lined baking tray and cook for 25 to 30 minutes until they look flaky on top best to undercook slightly rather than over cook as they could then lose the moist centre.

***

Crunchy Lemon Pie　　　　　**45 mins (ish)**　　　　　**Serve**

The Backstory

Our friend Yvonne Pass makes the best Lemon Pie in the business and after some persuasion she gave us her secret recipe. With four growing sons to look after (Henry, Jack, Freddie and Greg) she's a busy mum, so you can bet that all the recipes that she uses are easy to follow and reliable in their results!

The Gear

- 225g Ginger biscuits (crumbled)
- 110g melted butter or margarine
- 1 tin condensed milk
- Juice of 2 lemons
- Grated rind of 2 lemons
- 150mls fresh Double Cream OR Crème Fraiche (but not UHT)
- Crumbled chocolate flake (or other grated chocolate)

The Way

- Add the biscuit crumbs to the melted butter and stir well
- Place mixture into lightly greased pie dish (maybe line with foil)
- Leave in cool place or fridge to set - at least half an hour
- Place all the rest of the gear in a blender (mixer) blend/mix for 30 seconds
- Now pour in the cream and mix until incorporated
- Place the filling in the baking tin on top of the biscuit base
- Decorate with the "crumbliest chocolate in the world"
- Serve very chilled straight from the fridge

Biscuit crumbling?
Use a slow grinding action

Decorate with grated chocolate – Crunchy Lemon Pie

Traversing Tiramisu　　　**15 minutes + chillin' time**　**Serve**

The Backstory

Tiramisu means pick me up in Italian and this dish should give you more than a little "lift" with all the coffee and liqueur it contains.

The Gear

- 275ml fresh cold strong black coffee
- Two tablespoons Tia Maria or coffee liqueur
- 250g sponge fingers
- One medium egg separated
- 250g mascarpone cheese
- 35g sugar
- Two teaspoons coffee

The Way

- Mix liqueur with coffee and dip in half the sponge fingers one at a time
- Arrange the fingers in a single layer in a large dish
- Beat egg yolks with sugar until light in colour and gently beat in mascarpone until smooth
- In a separate bowl whisk egg whites and then slowly fold into the cheese mixture
- Pour half of the mixture over the sponge fingers
- Dip the remaining sponge fingers as in step 1 and arrange on top of the mixture
- Pour the remaining mixture over the top
- Smooth the top and then sprinkle with the cocoa powder
- Refrigerate for 24 hours before serving.

***

Snow Fruit Mogul   35 mins max   Serves 6

The Backstory

It's got to be said that some of us like Moguls less than others, but here's one that we have found popular with everyone. It's very difficult to ski round it; the best way to tackle this baby is to ski straight through it – with a desert spoon! It tastes great on its own, but even better with some vanilla ice cream.

The Gear

- 4 ripe juicy peaches (nectarines work just as well)
- 4 egg whites... – no yolks here ;-)
- 2 tbsp Madeira, or sweet sherry or lemon juice
- 270g light brown sugar / caster sugar
- 30g brown sugar

The Way

- Preheat the oven to 180 degrees Celsius
- Halve the fruit and remove the stones, then slice them all into ½cm slices
- Layer slices in a pyrex dish, or similar ovenproof container, sprinkle with brown sugar
- Now pour on the Madeira/sherry/lemon juice all over the fruit
- If you need to, you can soften the peaches up by whizzing them into the oven for 5 mins
- Whisk the egg whites in a bowl until the mixture becomes stiff
- Still beating, slowly add light brown sugar - continue to beat until stiff peaks appear
- With a large spoon, place meringue on top of the fruit mixture – make the top pretty!
- Bake in the oven for 15 or 20 mins or until the meringue is golden on top

***

Tarte Tatin **about 25-30 mins** **Serves 6**

The Backstory

Chalet Louis was built next door to an old Alpine farmhouse called Le Relais de la Dranse, which had been turned into a riding school and stables. During the summer the horses used to be turned out loose into the field at the bottom of our garden. Occasionally we hacked out with Monsieur Boufar the owner of the school, his wife Madame Boufar used to produce the most delicious, melt in the mouth Tarte Tatin – here it is. Ideal for packed lunches.

The Gear

- 2 cooking apples, or 4 peaches or 8 plums
- 2 tbsp brown sugar
- A packet of puff pastry
- Lemon juice

Le Tarte Tatin

at the oven to 220 Degrees Celsius

ut the pastry into a square

fold up the sides to form a uniform lip

e the fruit evenly and layer onto the pastry

rinkle the lemon juice liberally all over followed by the sugar

- Bake in the oven for 20-25 mins or until pastry rises and the top is caramelised
- Serve hot or cold with vanilla ice cream or fresh cream

***

Fakie Flapjacks   **25 mins max**   **makes 10**

The Backstory

This is a really easy one that even the kids will enjoy making – well ours do and they're fairly typical kids. Ideally let 'em cool right down before eating, (Erm... that's the flapjacks, NOT the kids!) Good for lunchboxes on the slopes.

The Gear

- 75g light muscovado sugar
- 3 tbsp golden syrup
- 150g rolled oats
- 75g unsalted butter

The Way

- Preheat oven to 170 degrees Celsius
- Put the butter, sugar and golden syrup together in a pan and melt very gently

- Then pour the melted mixture over the oats in a bowl and mix thoroughly
- Using a greased, shallow baking tray, (20x25cm) press the mixture down into it
- Now into the oven for 15 or 20 mins until it sets into a golden colour
- Allow to cool and then cut into squares

How they grow up, Mum & Hot Chocolate kid – Pg 94

9 THE OFF-PISTE RECIPES...

Approx 12 months   makes 1½ litres minimum

The Backstory................please drink responsibly.

Sloe... Sloe... Quick, Quick, SLOE! One of the nicest drinks to put in a hipflask and especially popular with the ladies, yes it's that old favourite of the hunting, shooting, fishing folk, Sloe Gin. The best thing about this Sloe Gin is that when you pass the flask round, you can say, "All my own work!" Sloe berries are the fruit of the blackthorn bushes which adorn British hedgerows and can be found in the autumn.

The Gear

- 1 kilo of Sloe berries
- ½ kg white granulated sugar
- Enough Gin to top up a 2L bottle

The Way

- The Sloes should be washed and then they need to have their skins split, either with a small paring knife or by putting them in the freezer until well frozen. The skins will split naturally and once thawed out, they can be put in the 2L bottle straight away
- Add the sugar, then top up with Gin close to the brim. When the cap is on the bottle, place it in a dark, cool cupboard
- Once a week you will need to take it out and shake the bottle to mix the contents and 3 months after you first put it in the cupboard, taste it to see if it needs more sugar
- Continue to leave it in the cupboard and it is recommended to leave for a year minimum, although there are those who are happy to drink it after 4 months. The mix improves with age and a good Sloe gin is often 2 years old

There's nobody more welcome on a long chairlift, than a skier who passes around a hipflask full of Sloe Gin – wonderful! In the evenings try it 50/50 with champagne – a Sloegasm... It can become addictive, you have been warned.

Gluh Wein   **30 mins tops**   **makes 8 small glasses**

The Backstory

For winter in the mountains, what a wonderful invention hot wine is? There are lots of different versions, Vin Chaud, Gluh Wein, Hot Mulled Wine etc. This is one we like the best and is a version of the Austrian speciality – Prost!

The Gear

- 1 bottle full bodied red wine
- 1 orange sliced – for garnish
- 100g golden caster sugar
- 300mls water
- ½ lemon, sliced
- 4 small sticks of cinnamon
- 10 cloves

The Way

- Stir the sugar, lemon and spices into the water in a small pan and simmer for 20 mins
- Take it off the heat and pour through a sieve into a larger pan
- Now add the wine and simmer for another 5 mins
- Ladle into cups or handled glasses and serve with a slice of orange in each one
- One sip and you will have died and gone to heaven!

***

Vin Chaud...to *GO!*   **20 mins**   **makes 6 glasses**

The Backstory

Another recipe for hot wine, this time using cardamom pods and nutmeg – variations on a theme eh? And jolly nice it is too!

The Gear

- One bottle of dry red wine
- 50mls Crème de Cassis (or Brandy)
- 100g caster sugar
- Finely grated zest of half a lemon and half an orange
- Large pinch grated nutmeg
- 2 sticks of Cinnamon
- 6 Cardamon Pods
- 6 Cloves
- Orange segments to serve

The Way

- Place all the gear in a saucepan, simmer gently don't boil it.
- About 10 mins later the flavours will have infused.
- Serve in warmed glasses with an orange segment in each.

***

10 APRÈS SKI

The following are some of our favourite **_après_** ski tipples. As with any pastime that requires a high degree of mental awareness and locomotor coordination, large amounts of alcohol and skiing do not mix well! It will all end in tears...

Warmed cider punch   **serves 4 -6**

100ml southern comfort or bourbon

Four crushed juniper berries

4 cinnamon sticks

One apple cored and sliced

660ml medium sweet cider

1.Put all the ingredients in to a pan and warm through

2. Remove the cinnamon sticks and serve

Cold start at Pré La Joux

Egg Nog   **serves 6-8**

Mostly served at Christmas or New Year egg nogs are rich but delicious and can be served slightly warmed or cold.

- 3 fresh eggs
- 3 tablespoons sugar
- Half pint milk
- Quarter bottle whisky
- Quarter pint dark rum
- Half pint whipping or double cream
- 2 tablespoons peach brandy
- Grated nutmeg

- Separate eggs putting the whites into a large bowl
- Beat yolks with sugar and quarter pint of the milk until smooth
- Pour into a punch bowl
- Add whisky stir in well then add rum and put to one side
- Whisk the egg whites until stiff
- Add the remaining milk, cream and peach brandy to the egg yolk mixture and stir in well
- Gently fold in the egg whites with a metal spoon until mixed in
- Serve in glasses sprinkled with a touch of nutmeg

End of the day's skiing – tired but happy

Hot Rum Punch   **serves 6-8**

- Juice three lemons
- One tablespoon sugar
- Half teaspoon ground ginger
- Quarter bottle brandy
- Half bottle dark rum
- Quarter bottle sherry
- 1 pint boiling water
- Grated nutmeg

- Pour lemon juice, sugar and ginger into a warm bowl and mix well
- Add brandy, rum sherry and hot water
- Stir and then serve with a sprinkle of nutmeg on top of each cup.

***

Irish coffee

- For each coffee you will need
- Hot strong black filter coffee
- Sugar
- One 25ml measure Whisky
- Double cream
- Take a heat proof glass and pour enough coffee to fill it a little more than half way.
- Add a teaspoon of sugar stir until it dissolves.
- Add the whisky and stir.
- Slowly pour a thick layer of double cream, over the back of a teaspoon, on to the top of the coffee so that it floats on top.

***

Cranberry warmer   serves 6-8

- 3 tablespoons instant lemon tea powder
- 350ml Orange juice
- 6 tablespoons sugar
- 1/4 tsp Cinnamon powder
- 1/4 tsp Nutmeg powder
- 900ml Water
- 500ml Cranberry juice

In large saucepan, combine all ingredients; heat through. Serve in cups or mugs and garnish, if desired, with a lemon or orange slice. Makes about 6 servings. This is a non alcoholic winter warmer but a dash of vodka or gin goes nicely if you wanted to add alcohol.

***

Jaeger Tee

This can be bought from many supermarkets in Switzerland and in some areas of France and Italy. It is pre mixed and just needs diluting according to the bottle instructions with hot water

Kaffee Fertig

This literally translates as finished coffee. It is a popular drink in Switzerland and is basically coffee with schnapps. My favourite is made with kirsch. Make up a glass of weak coffee either filter or instant and add a shot of kirsch and a spoon of sugar, stir and enjoy.

***

Fruity vodkas

- Large bag of skittles
- One 75cl bottle good quality vodka
- 5 empty small water bottles
- Or one large empty water bottle

First decide if you want to make 5 different fruity flavoured vodkas or one fruity mix vodka.

If making separate flavours separate the skittles into the five different colours.

Split the vodka evenly between the five bottles and add the individual flavoured skittles to each bottle. You will need approximately 50-60 skittles per bottle.

Then shake each bottle for 5 minutes and leave overnight until the rest of the skittles dissolve.

Once all the skittles have dissolved filter out the white gunk that will have accumulated on the top out through a coffee filter (you may have to filter twice) pour the filtered vodka into an appropriate container. Put in the freezer overnight and now they are ready to serve.

If you do not want to make the individual flavoured vodkas do the same process as above but in the large water bottle with the mixed flavour skittles the end result colour is not as attractive though. These flavoured vodkas are <u>very </u>strong and sweet so we recommend using mixers like diet cola, lemonade, ginger ale or soda water to dilute them.

***

Hannah's Mojito

Well what can we say about this one...? It is a cool, favourite cocktail, popular with all the family. Living in the heat (Athens, Greece) we tend to make these once in a while... In fact when we had a pool party at our house in the summer, Hannah was barmaid for the night and next morning when we counted up – she had made a total of 68 of them during the previous evening! Good effort Han ☺

Each glass contains:

- 2 tsp sugar
- 6-8 Mint leaves
- Soda Water
- 1 Lime halved
- 50ml White Rum – Bacardi does it for us

Put the sugar, mint and a little soda in a tall glass.
Muddle well (mash it all up) to dissolve the sugar.
Squeeze the juice from both halves of the lime
– drop one half in the glass
Add rum, stir well.
Fill with ice and top up with soda.

Athens – "twistin' by the pool" party

And the band played on...

ABOUT THE AUTHORS

James McBride - born in Chester, UK, the oldest of four sons. He always wanted to fly aeroplanes for a living since he was a little boy. On leaving school he worked as a Nurse, then had a career change in his twenties...

He joined the Royal Navy to fly jets and flew the Harrier and Helicopters before 'going civil' in the late 80's. He has been an airline Training Captain for many years and has written a book on flying called *The Flightdeck Survival Manual* – "How to survive a career flying aeroplanes for a living". It is available on Amazon.co.uk.

'The Flying Chef' was the owner of Chalet Louis in the French Alps for 10 years, from 1990. He is married with two children (Hannah & Lawrence) plus three dogs, currently living in Athens, Greece. Hobbies include; Cooking, Skiing, Watersports, Sailing, Diving and Motorcycling.

Mark Chetham – Mark Is from Chorlton in Manchester, he actually is, before it became trendy to claim so. As a young teenager in the 70's he would ask for curry instead of Sausages, or pizza instead of pie. His love of good, tasty food spans global cuisines, Asian, Ottoman, Greek, classic French, Iberian, rural English and Central European amongst his favourites.

He values good food, fine wine and great friendships. Always keen to share his enthusiasm for the perfect meal he found a kindred spirit in a neighbour and a pal, James.

Another joint passion was for skiing, and so one night in the idyll of the Haute Savoie, after a hard days skiing and a heady mix of wine, kirsch, Raclette cheese and quite probably more wine, they hatched the idea of sharing some of their favourite Alpine recipe ideas with friends, family and beyond.

Brothers and sisters together – sweet!

Was this the best day's skiing?

Was this the best day's skiing of our lives?

Did we ski a thousand turns today?

Wasn't the sun the brightest and snow the whitest?

Did we see a Trillion glittering diamonds in the snow and didn't that make us feel the richest?

Were the ski queues the shortest and queuing skiers the politest?

Was the sky not the bluest and our lines down the piste the truest?

Did we <u>really</u> ski a thousand turns today?

Were our Schusses the fastest and did our thighs burn the mostest?

Was the Vin Chaud the tastiest and the lunch conversation the liveliest?

Was the restaurant the roomiest?

Were the ski runs the smoothest and our ski jumps the longest?

Were the Pisteurs the friendliest and chairlifts the easiest?

Was today the best day's skiing of our lives and <u>did</u> we REALLY ski a thousand turns today?............................ *YES!*

**French Alps
Winter 2014**

Printed in Great Britain
by Amazon